CU00545988

"In these poems we see a man wh[o] embrace the world for its goodnes[s] joy. Nothing is immune from his c[_____] [_____] edges, round soft curves. He doesn't mealy mouth, doesn't primly curtsy; no, these poems remind me, in their gusto and awe, of my *tío* who used to tell stories sitting on his porch and during the telling slap his knee with emphasis for how much pleasure he got from the story — well, these poems have many knee slaps — enjoy, *amigos y amigas*, all of you who love poetry, these Christmas cookies and sopapillas come early."

– **Jimmy Santiago Baca,** author of *When I Walk Through That Door, I Am*

"Amidst these times of extraordinary chaos and turmoil, Price unfurls his treasure maps to the sublime so that we can 'fall in love with being alive.' If the weary, calloused heart is a geode, then Price's inimitable honesty is the sunlight for which our inner diamonds thirst."

– **Jenny Mason,** creator of the *Blister and Muck* mystery podcast

"Innocence Regained is an extraordinary collection. V. B. Price wrote these poems for Christmas each year from 1969 to the present. His magical ability to instill authentic childhood wonder with wicked humor and mature wisdom makes this book unique. And this is exactly what we need right now, as life careens about us, misery and violence on every horizon. I am stunned and often moved to a release of tears by the depth of this poet's humanity and the brilliance of his craft."

– **Margaret Randall,** author of *I Never Left Home: Poet, Feminist, Revolutionary*

"In New Mexico Christmas begins on the night before, when the weary and expectant are met with ancient hospitality and the path to every household is lit with candle-glow from humble paper bags. Faith holds that the greatest gift of all turned up in a manger when there was no room at the inn, and old folks know that this annual ritual seeks atonement for humanity's routine indifference and its rejection, long ago, of the incarnation of its own best impulses. Under cold stars, with the air made sacred from the incense of piñon fires, the hope of regaining lost innocence is renewed, and all comers are welcomed to the warmth of the hearth. Seeking that warmth, my wife and I joined the many others over the years who gathered at [the Prices'] house for wassail and conversation. Each year, we were all gifted with one of these poems — or with a lovingly handcrafted booklet containing a suite of them, five being a favored number. This is a poetry that ventriloquizes our own inner voice. It jibes and teases and coaxes us to pay attention to our better selves, seducing us with rare insights, wry humor, and irrepressible lyricism: 'Love is proof. It is in us / as light is in the stars.' It is the mind admonishing itself, spurring us to action, and providing comfort: '*a lo dado no se le da fin*' (to the gift no end is given)."

– **William Peterson,** former editor & publisher of *Artspace Magazine*

"Humane, deep, joyful, feral, challenging, beautiful, and always always always welcome. V. B. Price is a better poet than we deserve."

– **Daniel Abraham,** co-author of the *New York Times* bestselling series The Expanse

Innocence Regained

Other works by V. B. Price

Poetry
Memoirs of the World in Ten Fragments
Rome MMI
Broken and Reset
Death Self (with Rini Price)
Mythwaking
Chaco Trilogy
The Seven Deadly Sins
Documentaries
Semblances
The Cyclops' Garden

Nonfiction
The Orphaned Land
The University of New Mexico
Albuquerque: A City at the End of the World
Monsters (with Vincent Price)

Fiction
The Oddity

Innocence Regained

Christmas Poems

V. B. Price

Casa Urraca Press
ABIQUIU

Copyright © 2020 by V. B. Price

Foreword copyright © 2020 by Zach Hively

All rights reserved.

Thank you for supporting authors and artists by buying an authorized edition of this book and respecting all copyright laws by not reproducing, scanning, or distributing any part of it in any form without permission from the author directly or via the publisher, except as permitted by fair use. You are empowering artists to keep creating, and Casa Urraca Press to keep publishing, books for readers like you who actually look at copyright pages.

Cover image by Rini Price.
Set in Century Schoolbook and Journal Sans New.

First edition, v. 1.1

ISBN 978-1-7351516-2-5

CASA URRACA PRESS

an imprint of Casa Urraca, Ltd.
PO Box 1119
Abiquiu, New Mexico 87510
casaurracaltd.com

For Talia, Ryan, Jody, Amy, Keir, Helena, Toria, Chris, Deanna, Mercedes, Sophia, Susy, Mikki, Umea, Beckett, Erik, Miles, Jess, Kate, Clare, Gibb, Benito, Jonah, Juaquin, Luz, Brooke, Katherine, Rosemary, Serena, Jona, Logan, Jason, Evan, Sarah, Jenny, Eva, Denise, Zach, Daniel, Kat, Scarlett, Amaris, and Zane.

In memoriam
Rini Price

The Fezziwigs knew how to keep Christmas.

Contents

Foreword

My initiation into Christmas with the Prices took place under the dusk-shadow of the great cottonwood tree in the backyard. 'Twas the night before Christmas Eve when I braced with the poet V. B. Price at the far back door of their home. We slipped on leather gloves to protect our palms from sap, and also (I'm certain) because it was the manly thing to do. Rini Price and her accomplice conspired somewhere else to protect the house from an onslaught of piñon needles and wayward branches thrown like elbows.

The poet rubbed his wintry white beard, plotting our next several moves. He put one hand on the doorknob and, struck by the need to provide context, he put the other on my shoulder. "The next five minutes," he intoned, "are the closest we come to divorce every year."

I wish I could reveal the twinkle in his eye, or the mirth in his smile, when he warned me thus. I wish I could say it was all in jest. Anyone who knew this pair, so ravenously in love, would laugh off the story of that alert. But I was there, and I heard him say it like he was reciting an inscription over the vestibule of Hell.

That was it for preamble. We shot out the door, under cover of the cottonwood, to the magnificent young pine tree slurping water from a galvanized bucket. We sawed off the rump-end of the trunk and, like a team of Grinches in reverse, stuffed that tree into the house, through two quick right angles, and into what I call at all times of year the Tree Room.

Bless the two women indoors; they insinuated plastic sheets under us the whole way in vain. And such momentum! I did not help carry the tree into the Tree Room so much as the tree carried me. I was too afraid to let go.

The poet exaggerated only one line of his dire proverb: the whole shebang lasted a mere ninety seconds. With forty-plus Christmases together, the poet and the painter had whittled this annual strife from a Yule log to a Yuletide toothpick.

I am happy to report that this first Christmas Eve eve, as well as all the others I've been blessed enough to experience since, saw no casualties in the Prices' living room. No houseplants amputated from their pots, no paintings punctured by the tree bearers, no divorce papers procured. In fact, once we stood the tree in its stand and tied it to two hooks in the wall (a lesson taught before my time by a well-intentioned cat), Joy and Cheer reigned supreme. That great brief clash of Speed and Caution, I came to learn, cracked the seal on their own long-cultivated Christmas spirit.

Every year I am there for the celebration around the tree, I am the luckiest man in the world. One of the best moments — one of the things that has come to mean Christmas to me — is when the poet hands over a plain manila envelope, with my name in his distinct hand. I open it with the glee of a child who knows what he's getting from Santa and doesn't have to feign surprise. It's a small booklet, half-sheets of paper hand-stapled or hand-stitched together. It's a Christmas poem.

One of us asks the poet to read it aloud. He is delighted to. We nestle into our armchairs and couches, and in the quiet glimmer of the Christmas tree, of dear friends and a pure love, he reads.

Eventually someone or other is about to fall asleep, and we part ways. I always take my little book of poems to bed with me that night. Reading them again is my way of adding a second coat of Christmas, as it were. My way of bringing home the Tree Room, along with the smell of sap on my jeans.

The really beautiful thing about the Christmas poems is how freely the poet gives them away. I swear that everyone he can think of gets a copy, and he prints extras for the unexpected people he meets. That's how I got my first Christmas poems: we met for breakfast early one January before we were truly friends, and he pulled poems from his car and wrote a heartfelt note right there in the parking lot. Who does that these days — who but a real-life Santa Claus aspirant?

This chance to publish a selection of these Christmas poems, spanning from the very first one in 1969 to the very latest (so far) in 2019, is one of the delights of my existence. Everyone deserves the opportunity to feel the warmth of receiving these gifts. Everyone deserves to feel Christmas the way I get to — as a wildly sacred, fleetingly gorgeous expression of deep kinship and shared admiration.

My favorite poem of his (and perhaps, truth be told, my favorite poem in the world) is in this book. He mailed it to where I was attending graduate school. The same envelope as always, marked this time with a full address and too many stamps. That year's poem ends with lines that I would inscribe over my own vestibule, lines that inspire me beyond the days of Christmas:

The feral mind knows no bounds. Oh, do not tame it.

May you find your own such gifts among these poems.

Zach Hively

Introduction

As a feral child growing up in the 1940s and 1950s in Los Angeles, I knew of only one sure thing. As strange and scary as life could get, there would always be a Christmas miracle. I still believe it. Something beautiful and kind has always come along for me in late December every year for almost 80 years. Pure luck, I suppose. But we can't help making something out of what happens to us, no matter the source — Santa Claus, the gods of winter, the Snow Queen, the beautiful fates, who knows? On Christmas morning, I can always count on feeling like that William Blake etching of the "Glad Day" praising all. You know the feeling: a great glorious sunny morning taking hold of your body and soul. Did the spirit of Blake somehow infuse my development as a child, as I doggedly escaped the chaos of Hollywood scandals that engulfed my parents and threatened to take me down with them if I didn't flee to the safety of the beach and ocean any chance I got?

I wouldn't actually read Blake's poetry until the 1960s in an English class at the University of New Mexico. Only then did I realize the *Songs of Innocence* and *Songs of Experience* applied to my life as well as to everyone else's. For me, innocence had left far too early, and I wrestled with the ordeals of experience the best I could. It was only at Christmastime that I experienced what I've come to think of as "innocence regained." It's a rare state of being. For most of us, it's received momentarily as a re-experiencing of the wisdom of children as it's embodied in their capacity for surprise and delight without inhibition. Innocent merriment is the partner of innocence regained.

The first time I remember experiencing such a feeling, I was seven. I was worried. My parents were unhappy with each other. I could feel it. But they were committed to making a final family Christmas for me and for themselves, one that might carry us through the crucible of a Hollywood divorce. I had a cold that Christmas, and it kept me in bed.

To make me feel better, they lavished me with comic books rolled up and tied with red ribbons, and with the love they wanted to, but no longer could, lavish on each other. Innocent merriment was the rule of the season. My parents still had moments when they became again children at heart, full of fun and excitement and a delight in life. And that Christmas my terrible worries about them, and my horror that I might have caused them to be unhappy in some unimaginable way, were dispelled in a regaining of deep safety and happy surprise. Years later my mother still filled a nylon stocking full of oranges, nuts, and presents every Christmas morning. Presents were always piled under the tree, even when she didn't have the money. She'd tell stories of her mother and father, weathering for a moment the death of their beloved first son, Lawrence, in the battle of Bellow Wood in World War I. Christmas — its traditions and rituals — gave them strength before they both could no longer endure their grief. Ever a man looking for joy, my father, too, loved the merriments of the season. I remember trailing behind him in shops full of jams and cookies and delicatessen delectables in little jars and tins. Those stores lodged in my memory as miniature Aladdin's Caves, overflowing with sumptuous and glittering delights.

Three years after that last Christmas with my parents together, as a ten-year-old, still afraid of what one of my peers had told me was the fate of kids from divorced families — the orphanage — I met and I suspect "fell in love" with an eccentric neighbor, a grandmotherly woman who rode a blue bicycle she named Nadine. She kept flotillas of desert turtles and myriad other critters on her two adjacent lots in Santa Monica. I thought she was the best grown-up I'd ever known, and she loved children and festooned them with lingonberry jams and bisquits, and tall tales of the exploits of cats with names like Oberon and Titania. In 1950 she invited me to "star" in her Christmas play that year and play the part of Pixie Joyheart. I still have the little card inviting her friends to the performance of "Christmas Joy" in her distinctive exuberant broad line handwriting. On the corner of the card is a paste-on silver star. On the back it reads "Collection

'Care.'" The performance was in her barn. She'd had it built as a home for her magical horse, Sleipnir, named from the eight-legged, winged white steed of Odin. The good burghers of Santa Monica had decided, though, that a horse didn't fit the zoning code. Inside the barn that night everything was lit with candles so the whole room sparkled through the incense. By the stage was a white wooden rocking horse, a tiny Sleipnir with a basket for donations. Only many years later did I come to see the inside of the barn as like the inside of a geode just opened, so dazzling and surprisingly beautiful it throws one out of experience and into a kind of innocent awe at the raw splendor of it.

Soon after "Christmas Joy," the natural world began to reveal itself to me in ways that felt loving and generous, like a child's theater of amazements. Gulls, pelicans, tide pools, sea anemones, driftwood, breezy sunny mornings where your shirt felt like a sail filling out, the glorious smells of breakfast at the beach, finding smoothed shell fragments and even smoother stones that I could hold in my hand, keep in my pocket, and make my own.

Then in the early 1960s I had a divorce of my own, which I had vowed I would never do. My children were taken out of state. I've never felt so desolate in my life. I started to think my Christmas luck had run its course and that I was doomed to the world of humbug, Scrooge-ism, and bleak experience, the dismal boredom of an American commercial Christmas. I was about to turn my back on my own history of good fortune. And then my first geode appeared. I was 24 and I'd never seen one before. A friend brought it by my apartment in Old Town to cheer me up on Christmas Eve. It was in a brown paper sack. She held it up at the door and said, "Here's a Christmas miracle for you." I still have it, of course. A round, rough, gray, grapefruit-sized ball with a huge hole in it as if a planet had exploded from the inside. And there I saw bewilderingly gorgeous, glowing hidden crystals glistening in the light like the essence of winter in my hand. No, my luck had not run out.

That geode started me on a hunt for the "beauties of the cosmos," a term I never liked but could never improve.

It became a Christmas mission every year. I discovered rock shops, dozens of them all over the west, from Byram, Montana, to Carrizozo, New Mexico, and points in between. Nothing was more fun than going through boxes and caches of minerals looking for magical configurations in stone — fluorite crystals, pyrite-replaced brachiopods, azurite-encrusted landscapes the size of a fist, fossil fish, fossil feathers, round rocks of any kind, wish-stones from the ditch with bands of different colored minerals around them, fossil cephalopods, badger claws, sharks' teeth, the golden section in spirals of stone, the ocean green of marcasite — and then wrapping them up and giving them to friends and children on Christmas Eve at our house in the North Valley of Albuquerque.

Presents like that can be gateways to bursts of awe and sweet humility at the wonders and mysteries of the world, like when one of my sons on his eighth birthday got a hammer and a rock wrapped up in a pretty box. He looked puzzled and slightly askance. "Hit the rock with the hammer." He did. It bounced off. He did it again and again. He was about to give up when with one last mighty whack the rock split in half and he literally gasped with glee at the bedazzlement of crystals glowing inside. I'll never forget that moment. It was the essence of a joyousness that's still possible for each one of us, if we want it enough to allow our defenses and sophistications to rest for a while so we can greet the world with our curiosities, ready to be surprised and fascinated by secrets of the world we hardly look at day to day.

Innocent merriments can also turn slightly impish when surprising wonders are just too bizarre not to find funny. Many years ago in a Santa Fe trading post that still catered to Pueblo people, I found a stash of stuffed ravens to be used in ceremonies. They had white cotton eyes and were wrapped in Chinese newspapers from, I was told, Taiwan. I bought ten and sent them as rare surprises to friends I thought would be as amused as I was. No one ever mentioned them. Not too long after, undeterred, I was in Golden and found a little shop of oddities that had on its upper shelves what looked like baby food jars with smiling baby labels. They seemed incongruous in such a place and when I asked about them, the woman behind the counter said, "Reach up and take a look." Inside the little jar with a baby cooing over strained peaches, I saw an enormous coiled centipede, preserved in formaldehyde! The woman's long thin face scrunched up in laughter. I bought a dozen of them, $2.50 a piece I think, with tarantulas, wasps, little snakes, scorpions. "Oh, you know all manner of little critters try to chisel you out of your food around a place like this," she said. "The husband knows how to get um." I gave them to special friends that Christmas Eve with shrieks around the tree before they got their redeeming rocks.

I'm not sure why I got it into my head on my first Christmas with Rini, my late wife, to write a Christmas poem each year that would come to me, as it turned out, where all poems come from — "the secret life of making new things." Their writing is truly more an act of transcription than of creation, though everything always needs the hand of the journeyman to make the joinery smooth enough to be entertaining. I've written such "occasional" poems every Christmas ever since, usually under strenuous time constraints. Family and friends have said they cheer them up. So I kept on writing them, and will keep on as long as the years permit.

Innocence Regained

Christmas License

When you come to our house this Christmas
open the little jars.
You are free to have whatever you find:

the shadows of eagles in cellophane sacks,
a stack of arthritic rain;
     all your thoughts on a microdot;
a slab to the Sundance Sea;
     Goethe's bad breath over sensible gossip and gooseberry wine;
a primer on Mayan subjunctives;
     that wind the first morning you broke from her bed;
Long John Silver's confidence.

You are free to have whatever you find.
Our pleasure, indeed. But please,
be kind to Jesus and Jude, look for the truth,
take liberties with your mind.

(1969)

Necessary Quality: A Gift

We are never poor of luxury
      while in sympathy with quality,
with craftsmanship, restraint and thrift,
      and careful durability —
the common eccentricities
      abundant in our poverties.
So, if you still believe in giving gifts,

in Christmas gifts, ingenious gifts,
in generous, genial gifts
      like bone,
your big present, then, from us this year will be
      your own most bountiful
and merry body, offered temptingly,
      breathing happily beneath your tree; and you

responding to this luxury
      with gracious curiosity.
A gift's sole pleasure
      is in having all its mysteries released
in use, in gratitude,
      in thoughtful Will renewed.
So, if you still believe in giving gifts

release your body
from at least *one* boring truth this year
      by being so inspired, so intrigued
as to feel beneath the wrapping
      to violate appearance
by handling the goods,
      exploring

underneath your face, your wrists,
      your fingers, arms and feet,
releasing, genial to your consciousness,
      your own considerate
and confidential bone —
      so diligent, devoted,
compulsory and lavish.

In other years,
I would have brought you tapir skulls,
      bear toes, the spines of newts,
or lizard bones —
      a million, billion lizards
and not a sloppy vertebra,
      each one fits —
to intrigue your generosity,
      to lavish you with quality,
with craftsmanship, restraint, and thrift,
      and careful durability:
with beauty
      that functions
beautifully.

But this poor year,
I can only just afford our own,
      our own slow bones,
so kind, so patient,
      so presumed upon,
neglected,
      misinterpreted, and slandered:

"Skull and Cross Bones,"
        the cheapest cut of all.
Our own skulls!
        how meanly we misuse them,
those ingenious,
        caring functions, those
reliquaries

that still preserve
(in our Will to give,
        to trust and work)
the purpose of that Confidence
        that caused the light
that aspired to our eyes
        that last silent night

that last saw God
        complete, at last,
        his last kind thought
        before the next.

(1970)

Taking Sides

"There is nothing solid, nothing still or understood
in all the world." And though I'm one of many, and we're all to
    blame,
I am not humbled by the stars when I stare alone into the
    midnight sky.
They make me proud that I'm alive, as distant as I am,

that even in the starlight on the surface of my eyes,
our matter is the same. I'm just as much the star's terrain
as they're the outer stillness of my brain. It is a necessary vanity
to claim them. And if we share a purpose, what questions I give back

to the hungry space, for which we thrive, are at least no less
than all the lessons of their private grace. Though I would agree
that when a starlight dies, if I should live to see it,
it would be, in my own eyes, greater even than my death

but, by the holy trouble of the human mind,
not the deaths of all my kind.

(1973)

New Catacombs

We who live in a disintegrating time,
     who are that time,
we for whom so little is holy,
     the self-made ones, where do we belong,
useless as we are, but underground,
     within: intimate, alone,
but with each other?
     For moral wanderers like us,

bereft of revelation,
     there's only love to trust,
that halo of beloveds,
     those with whom we've shared
the bliss of honesty, conspiring to know,
     those without whose truthfulness
our selves would be half known to us,
     to them and them alone do we belong.

In this numb time of emptiness and lies,
     there's little else to do
but hood our eyes, take refuge in reflection,
     and when we do
we find them there, our patron friends,
     like stars
within our skulls, a firmament of angels
     igniting faith again

in what we are, our minds new catacombs,
     each one of us a shrine,
a secret place in which to love is holy
     and the bliss of honesty divine.

(1974)

Lovers and Prophets

What a brutal place,
this beautiful and generous place:
cruelty, accident, sudden death and war,
the random horror of this life
rational as tumors.
Do you remember how it was before,
how aware of it we were,
smothered in our terror and its scars,
excluded from the rest of all that was?
But that was all before that night, for me,
in the wilderness of stars, staring at those perfect,
terrible deep lights, their patterns in the vaulted dark
like brain paths of the Universe evolving, glorious, divine,
and yet so intimate and kind.
It was loving you that I recalled that night.
In memory, the heavens had become my mind.
It was then I understood those mysteries, artificially alive,
paralyzed in gospels, idols, history and lies,
and I said in triumph what I knew: "Through you, beloved,
I have loved the stars, and belonged to them
through you."
For that moment, loving had transformed me from a tomb of scars
to a prophet who could say, with lovers, the Universe is ours.

(1975)

Being Present

So much is missing now,
so much is taken from us.
We define our lives by absences,
by cannot-haves and contradictions,
by choices impossible to choose.
And oh our opal sufferings,
the pining for our fantasies —
the lovers, absolutes, utopias —
that ever have come true.
Heavy with our vacancies,
possessed by what is not,
we are not present at our lives,
but locked within discrepancy
until some shock, some generosity,
a living moment absolute with evidence,
penetrates our absences,
turns us inside out
and presses us against
the simple presence of the world,
and we feel inside us
what is all around us,
give ourselves to what is there,
a relief so deep
we know ourselves for what we are:
totalities of moments
that have to be enough.

(1976)

Endurance

The wind adored her;
seaweed, doorways, alleys, bees — all things
sought pleasure in her praising eye:
      this slug of a person,
      mute as a stump,
      untouchably gray,
trolling around downtown every day
searching for coins and shade.
The storekeepers smiled
      when Rosalie came, but none ever saw
past her crumpling hobble, none could have known

that long, long ago, when she first
knew she would be
all alone all her life,
      she turned her appearance
      into a wall, made of herself
      a secret retreat, resolving not
to be less than she was,
but to be what she felt, to try
to love each thing that she found,
      to love the whole world if she could,
on the vague chance that it mattered.

She never gave in,
this crust of a person
hidden in scabs and shawls.
      Excluded herself,
      she included all things,
      made room for tenements, stones and mold,
for faces and spiders and bones and trees,
examining each
particular beauty
      admiring all
as relics of grace.

Rosalie's life hummed with the effort,
the miracles all
in harmony there:
      her hobble a dance,
      their ritual form,
      a pattern of care.
She wouldn't let up, giving herself
and the world every chance.
The traveling dance is what saved her.
      She faltered as often as anyone else,
knew the numb panic of doubt,

the razor and stink of self-pity, but these
were merely caesuras,
flaws in the pulse of the strength she'd create
      from disciplined time. This rhythm, persistence,
      evolving momentum,
      carried her over
each fatal pause. And hunched in doorways,
pushing her way through storms and grime,
she endured to the end,
      each second of life adding up
until one day

she felt she'd become
the planet itself,
sublime, and full, and loved.
      When Rosalie died, medical
      students routinely
      shaved off her hair, sawed into her skull,
but when
they opened her head
they found
      an unaccountable glow,
"almost a halo," one of them said.

Astonished,
they searched through her cells for answers and saw
what looked like branches of lights
      patterned throughout, decked
      with uncountable moons and stars.
      Most chose not
to believe what they saw,
but shaking his head, one of the students,
who'd seen her downtown, added a note
      to the tag on her toe:
"St Rosalie," it read.

(1977)

Details from a Season's Greetings

The impressions came like this:
first sea
then greet,
then ocean gray,
then twilight on the waves, ash cold,
then chimney smoke,
forest dark
the morning house,
ice sky
slippery in the wind.
Halo at the window, pearly cold,
the tree
black green, freezing
ankle shadows,
coffee smoke, hands and knees, groping, then,
oh then, oh instantly Times Square,
Aurora Borealis in the corner!
Mind lights all
opal butter hugs, warm cheeks and shawls,
Pinocchio and Bing, then
snow light, silent gray,
side by side, wind in pines,
lichens rocks roots loam,
breath clouds
in the dell,

mountain kids
in Hebe's house,
its cape of firs
and fishing fogs, live bait, bay rum, breakfast
up the coast with Dad, the hook
behind the eye, blue plate special, primal brine,
twilight walk back from school, late, first time,
fear replaced
by lights inside, sweet pride, stories to tell, soup
in the diner,
hot rolls' steam, windows glazed,
black night, waves, pastry green
holly leaves, painted
backward "Season's Greetings"
facing to the sea.

(1978)

Untitled

perfect
clear light
star mind
chorus
eye star
joyous
pulse light
clear
nerve star
pulse sight
heart bright
chorus
joyous, joyous
all one light

perfect
clear light
star mind
chorus
eye star
joyous
pulse light
clear
nerve star
pulse sight
heart bright
chorus
joyous, joyous
all one
light

perfect
clear light
star mind
chorus
eye star
joyous
pulse light
clear
nerve star
pulse sight
heart bright
chorus
joyous, joyous
all one
light

*[Note: The first stanza is to be spoken,
the second is to be chanted,
the third is to be sung.]*

(1979)

Changing

for Marjorie Herman Rini, 1914-1980

> *... just once,*
> *everything, only for once.*
>
> – R. M. Rilke

Icons of change, mortality,
the coming and the going,
this here and now... now,
there is your smiling,
your healing smile,
your serious frivolity as whimsey's sage;
in the face of evil or of pain,
your Cheshire form crusading,
adding, as you said we must,
love to the way things are.

Your presence now
diffused through time
permits to empty, grim dark
self-escaping.
The humor in death
is that it's all over,
is that it is not
its sadness to be escaped.

To escape, belong,
love change,
belong to what does not remain,
the coming and the going,
the crow noise, windshine,
gust light through the leaves,
green wind morning shade,
ripples of the muskrat,
of vanished seas on canyon stone,
the brittle valleys in the clay
leached up from rain,
your smiling, gallant toddling
... love does not preserve,
it knows;
it is enough.
The humor in death
is that it's all over,
as your presence is
your smile; your gift to us
this here and now, this once
that is this Christmas almost past.

(1980)

In Praise

> *... For every day they die*
>   *Among us, those who were doing us some good,*
>   *And knew it was never enough but*
>   *Hoped to improve a little by living.*
>
>   – W. H. Auden

And what would the star shine down on now? The same
follies of venality, deceit, that's sure; the humor,
panic, savagery's the same, and too
the piety of torturers, truthmongers and their crimes, but now
a comic horror rules: would-be world assassins, not
robot fanatics but the world's "great men,"
contrive to sabotage all human time, they
and their lunatic science that spawns
anarchic switchery, a life zone of cannibal contraptions
on which we must depend, a dooming gizmosphere
triggering the fusion of idiot polarities, and
as then, the insolence of cynics, of practical men who proclaim
peace naive, good faith unrealistic, but
who do so now like varmint kids kill dogs
for the inevitable fun of little evils.

In New Mexico this winter,
in the desert of our contradictions, our
target solitude, this
most remote, most unsuspected of places where
temptations to the absolute and elemental were
grandly accepted, we walk the land in twilight,
among the sand hills, scrub, the purity of cold, old cottonwoods,

proud to be alive, and in the dark pearl water
of the river pools we see: Venus, moon clouds,
maternal night, the star itself
riding on the breeze waves, hard-brilliant,
self-contained, an evidence of vastness in which
all things are — photons, river toads, precision
instruments that maim, and
the ardor, kindness, joyful trust
that takes hold of us in beauty or in love.

And we are here
among the things that are, the desert
of our contradictions, possibility in us
as varied as the evidence of stars,
free enough at least
to feel no shame to act in praise of peace,
at least to speak against the cynic deathmen,
at least that much, which is
not enough, but does
improve somewhat the chance
for a little more living.

(1981)

The Calling

Lovers of finity,
of sea form, crystals,
breakfast light, and wings,
of motion, moon shade
and the disappearing stars,
of all things particular,
we are not the fossils, fat extinctions,
of some end time now;
we are what is next.
Lovers of bodies, rivers
of lifetimes, and of pines,
of lightning, cities, and the air,
the past, through us, can be
a future that is not
the suicide of time.
Lovers of sandstorms and of winter rooms,
of child life, crane flight, and the hills,
lovers of ice, the wind, and eyes,
the visions have been sent,
the prophets, holy sages
have come and gone;
we are what is left.
There is a waiting now to see
if we're the ones,
in saving multitudes, who are
heirs of those who knew
that lovers are
one and the same
with what they love.
Lovers of dawn chill, gyres,
of galaxies, and noon
it is our time to know,
as they once knew,
that brain light and the stars
are the same hard mortal fire.

(1982)

Reversing the Fall

for Chris who took us there

> *I swear the earth shall surely be complete to him or her*
> *who shall be complete.*
> *The earth remains jagged and broken only to him or her*
> *who remains jagged and broken.*
>
> – Walt Whitman, "A Song of the Rolling Earth – No. 3"

At Canyon de Chelly,
at its infinite edge,
looking down, ten thousand feet down, overcome,
opened before its untouchable grace,
forbidden,
its visible fields, far meadows, and groves,
its terranean stream,
safe, far away,
so far away, exultantly far, that its grace
becomes our desire;
and the stories we tell to ourselves,
the lives we would live there,
our longing for dawns on the floor of the deep,
in the mind of the place, canyon walls guiding
light through the brain.
At the infinite edge, the urge is to fly,
to embrace what is seen... but the fall,
the mortal distinction,
the death between flesh and world.
We walked
down into de Chelly that day, actually down, descending
into desire, and
into the real canyon we'd seen,
reaching the stream, our real feet in the mud,
swifts in the air above us, sky above them,

actually there, there with our bodies,
our real nerves touching the rock, the water;
we were
what we'd desired, our brains filled with the place
and what we had made of the place, together
reversing the Fall.
At the farthest part of ourselves
we'd disappeared into de Chelly;
the distance had opened
out into that place in the self
no longer the self, but complete,
as one might glance at the morning star and know
no distance exists between eyes and light,
between light and brain,
between stars and the self's earthly night.

(1983)

Openings

*With all its eyes the creature-world beholds
the open...*

     – R. M. Rilke

As children we knew
animals were strangers who were like us,
distant in their fur as history and gods,
yet filled with needs, with mysteries and will
as given as our own,
their eyes pure portals
to the mind of atoms and its things,
as our eyes were
openings of the world.
   Gliding now with age,
half blind, half free,
our child sight still divine inside us,
we know the world as friend
when we can trust
animals to be, like us, only what they are,
not what we would have them be.
    Irreplaceable, gone almost as we appear,
creature things who love,
who know the love itself if not the lover,
we make the far unknowing of each other
as intimate as stars in dreams
that lead the child in us
to watch what is, to see it
as it is, to see ourselves that way,
absolute as sun, as pain, as animals, as night,
as the fact and proof of love
that gives us sight.

(1984)

Doing Who We Are

Old children of beauty,
old children of pain,
knowing what has come before
the child-light tree that claims us,
chosen for our joy,
we know we are alive now,
looking past our fear,
free as the tree
radiant with paradox,
alive and good as dead.
Old children,
feral with the jokes of self,
we have hewn the tree from the land,
bear its cutting as next of kin —
monsters and angels of sacred play,
unsure of gift
or violation —
and feel with it still, not knowing if it feels
this celebration, its green delight
in our delight as we obey
the secret will in us
to be released from ice,
to trust our impulse to the light,
adorn the forest with our holy toys,
our lives with the passion of its windy nights.
Old children, chosen for our joy,
we stand with the tree,
it stands for us,
for that true known
we sense in us through childhood trust
that fun
is heavenly
and good.

(1985)

Talisman

a year of weather
globed into a disc
the alchemy of noticing
with magical effect
the optimum
and optimism
filling up the space between
doubt and faith
judgment
dread
dismissed
the attitude of feathers
slowly fitted to the best
on the current of necessity
and everywhere the charm
the source of luck
everywhere
the optimum
and optimism
globed into a disc
to practice with
the alchemy of weathering
habits of dejection
self-defeat
spinning love from dust
roaring
flying
practicing reversal
with magical effect
everywhere
the talisman that spins
the axis of reflection
opting
ego
into laughter,
cages into velds

(1987)

In Praise of Friends and All Beloveds

Near death in darkness,
frozen in an ice-wake
of a hate that grief aborted,
I stared out from my body's grave
into the closed eyes of the night

and became the object of a star
so far and cold I feared its light
would leave me with no shadow.
But as I shrank into my pain,
by grace of mind, I thought of you.

And as I did, the star,
that far dead light of gasses in the void,
came all alive. All night was living,
the universe itself was all alive in me.
The grace of love remembered

freed me from the grief of hate,
the little graces of self and species.
And I could see that I belonged
to all the light that was alive.
I am as much of what the night sky is

as a nova I can never see.
My grief does not hunger in a void,
in a universe of beauty that is dead.
Love is proof. It is in us
as light is in the stars.

It is a property of atoms
as comets, trees, and questions are.
Because of you, I knew we are alive
within a universe that loves.
My life is not a filling grave of loss

in a freezing splendor without sense.
Through you, I saw
love makes the universe alive.
And with the warmth of that belonging,
I survived the night.

(1990)

Starlight in the Woods

for Ryan Keir Price, b. July 13, 1994

> *Yet as a wheel moves smoothly free of jars,*
> *My will and my desire were turned by love,*
> *The love that moves the sun and other stars.*
>
> — Dante, *Paradiso*

There is no map to guide us through the forest,
    no homing echoes through the void,
        no comfort in the urge of data
        extruding without end or purpose.

We've looked and looked for something obvious,
    some rule to guide us,
        something that made sense of Hitler
        and his smiling mother.

And we've learned it's useless to stay confused.

The guide
is
a gift.

It wasn't hiding
in the tracklessness of chance.

It was with us all along,
    we've learned,
        with us in our arms,
        in the faces of our children,
        in our lovers' eyes,
    before us across a table,
        in the voices of our friends,
        in our love of rocks, and stars, and weather,

in all
    mysterious affections.

How we see is what we see,
    we've learned.

Effortless, I see you.
You give me ease,
    an ease to follow,
        a guiding clarity
        in mires of distraction,
        a truthfulness
            beyond The Truth.

Like the absolute
true impulse
to take a breath,
    I look at you
    and find my way
        by just
        the sight of you
  — your smile
        the midnight sky
        holy and windy with eternities of stars.

(1994)

from Five Gifts

I. The Shadows of Pens

I was thinking of gifts
when the shadow of my pen point on the page
seemed ominous and strange with meaning

and recalled to me all the women and all the men
who had given all their breath and all their hope
just to hold up a few honest words

in the face of the great
joyless snarl
that wanted them still, so still

they would be like snow falling on snow,
all of them compressed into a white noise, so flat, so blank
it turns to vapor, soundless with the slightest heat.

I saw my pen point moving on the page
and felt in myself the lifetimes of ink
living through hands that move pens
so eyes can find thoughts
rising like words from mist across mountains.
And I saw myself as a whisper of light

in that luminous flow of shades
that moved the shadow of my pen point on the page,
and saw that I was, myself, being written

by their desire to write,
those so many lives, bright-gifted and destroyed.
And I couldn't help but hear pens all around me

scratching out words from prisons and graves,
and I knew what I owed them — the starved, the tortured,
the failed, the hanged, the far, thunderous
whisper of their ink as it flows illumined from lives into lives

— I owed them everything, even my faith, even my desire.
My life had become their gift to me, as we all are gifted
by the flow of air, of passion, of courage, of brave delight.
As I saw my pen point and its shadows
draw my life on the page before me,

I felt myself outgrow myself,
grow invisible and safe in the crowds of the defiant,
and I knew I would never write words on a page again

and feel alone, that the shadow of their will,
their refusal to be still
would not desert me — that shadow like a burn,

like age, would never wash away in sunlight or in fire,
in the lamplight in my room, or the ash light
of a dungeon's moon ... I was thinking of gifts.

(1995)

For Talia Sandra Price

— on her first Christmas

I know three gifts
no one can give you.

First, the kind of knowledge a bird needs
to trust the air with itself,
        the kind of ease that you will need
        to entrust yourself to your strength.

Second, the kind of humor the dying need
to entrust their hope to pain,
        the kind of fearlessness that you might need
        to dream yourself sane in a war.

Third, the kind of peace the self-fulfilling always need
to reject the cruel in the cause of kindness,
        the kind of dignity you will need to question yourself
        when you're burning with the certainty of right and wrong.

These the world won't give you as it tests you.
You will have to find them on your own, and as you do,
        the gift of your growth will become
        the gift that your life gives to everyone else, even to me.

(1996)

Five Epiphanies of Letting Go

I. Just Like That

Liberty from fear, that clearest happiness,
can happen just like that, fast as ice
returns to water, as water lifts itself
from weight, vaporous with luck.

You never know exactly when, but just like that the neural world
is radical delight, chains evaporate, stains come clean,
the glue of dread is drained, long struggles fade, and hopeless goals
welcome you without restraint. Who can calculate? This
      sudden, free

deep breathing, after smothering in disbelief,
is nothing to expect. We can only wait alert,
so trusting of our chances never to desert us

we make room for nothing we can know
until it comes to us in wild relief like fate,
and for once, like that, we are not too late.

II. Not Fallen After All

Self-knowledge turns out to be
like blowing dust from a shell one day and finding it
all radiant pure pleasure, like fogging up a jasper globe

and rubbing it on your shirt until
the magnificent insignificance
of its details can't be missed.

Nothing in the universe is flawed. So we
are not, at heart, less than we are,
quantum misfits dirty with mortality,

in need of thumbscrews, dungeons, moral spies
to conform us to opinions that force has turned to lies.
We're not like that after all. It's not our fault we die.

Coming clean is simple as a puff of breath, a single choice
to hear our pains and truths in another's breath and voice.

III. Who First Treated You Like a Person First?

We're all curiosities, more or less,
lonely in some universal way
unique to us, isolated in our mirrors,
freaks of beauty, freaks of wealth,

freaks of fame, of gossip, or our sex;
freaks of poverty, or class, or brains,
of clothes, or teeth, or awful hair. But then,
just once, at first, we see that we are to someone else

just who we are to ourselves. We're stunned. They love us,
despite what they know of us. And fear escapes us;
there's nothing, now, we can't reveal, even privacies aren't secrets.
This is a miracle we never forget. It's in our bones, this peace

that comes with being known, this gift that let us look beneath
our fear of ourselves and gave us a life to keep living.

IV. We're So Afraid of What They'll Say

We can't help hiding.
It's cleaner than lying, our logic sneers,
like craving the noose when we're drowning.
Most of the time we are missing.

We've disappeared so well, we can't even escape,
snared by our own camouflage,
startled horribly awake, forgetting who we are,
frantic to take a chance, to jump headfirst

into the head of someone else, sick with worry
they'll step aside, drum their fingers, let us fall
into the hell of their garbage-disposal judgment calls.
Oh wake up! Let go! They're all as scared as we are.

Listen to their fear. Let it track you down,
hear it and you'll be heard.

V. Giving Joy Away

All this worry, all this inward scheming,
all this vivisection of ourselves, our molasses longings,
our wicked little shame

of exactly how we look, all our habits of fret
that screw us down so tight our heads break off from the stress.
But that old man over there, he never worries

about being old and so close to death,
never worries as a motive or distraction;
he never worries the sleigh won't fly.

Gently, gently he sees himself rising, lifting up and soaring,
giving and giving without worry until
he gives himself all away, like time gives away

all its sweet days. Could there be
anyone more fulfilled than he?

(1997)

Paradox Presents

I.

Erasing from your net of nerves
all distractions of despair and stress
can be as effortless as sprouting
roses from your finger tips.

Life's a trick the boxer said, a sleight
of thought, a nimble here and there, easy as kids can make
skipping seem like flying.
Old age boring through your life

cannot compete with happy bafflements
spilling lilacs from the snow, even the animal
sadness of being hated, the dizzy sweats of a life
you love and cannot help that tips you over day after day,

cannot compete with the alchemy of chance that makes
the mortality of every moment so much more than enough.

II.

The junk store twirls and sparks with stars, becomes
a myth of the marvels of plenty.
Toasters, highboys, creamers, owl and pussy cat

salt and pepper shakers, costume treasures worth a ransom of candy,
dented pots and stained pans, worn tools like gorgeous hands,
    long stemmed
ashtrays, loved toys of every kind cascade

like diamonds, wishes, pearls from Ali Baba's cave.
Cranes call loud enough, sometimes, to wake the dead
end in us so sunlight startles us like dawn escaping through

orange nasturtiums on the window sill without a moral,
and you see your own wild eyes as lights in an empty place
on the map of night and know where you are at last.

Being found is as simple as losing your place. And in the meantime,
every moment is so much more than enough.

III.

Slick river stones round as caressing,
hawks swooping, we know, for mice who might
escape out of sight, haters turned into dust
devils like tornados drooping
into soggy drafts, our neural net of stars
can change their constellations

faster than surprise; breathing in and out
amazes us as much as the warm, sweet mulled
misgivings we feel in the absence of the fear of death;
around our brains the star rose and heavens of the angels of
      our lives,
those magicians of sweet luck who give us to ourselves because
they love us only as we are, their gifts to us are like

choirs of laughter from worn kids who sense
every moment is so much more than enough.

IV.

Pain dominates our neural nets,
its usefulness, like fear's, is undisputed.
We're alerted, and we might survive
in this sumptuous place where living means
eating other life, where what we most adore

cyclones into trash on vacant seas,
where loving can expire in killing so preposterously vast
no one can remember why, where germs use us as food,
where weather in its normal flux
can obliterate our cache, our citadels, our temples

like blowing dust from stones. Is this some kind of hell,
the magician of paradox a devil in a cheap disguise? No, it's just
a trick of fact. We see through it when we sense that every moment
is all there is and so much more than enough, if we just believe it.

V.

Inside makes the outside every time.
Cats billowing with silly speed, or slow like cold honey on the
prowl,
bat bones so perfectly uplifting in the sheerness of their beauty
that bats can fly,

being childish with our pleasure, under penalty of death,
we thrive on what the Rule of Food, that ball and chain of all
eating all,
finds quite superfluous: the cosmic triviality of happiness and
feeling good,

which lurks more secret and ever present just behind our luck
than all the normal wickedness of fear and blank disaster
known by pain.
Once we learn the trick, that subatomic particles combine and
so relate

to create a planet or a thought, that love is a property of life
which is itself a property of light, that we are made of the same
space time in which the cosmos now unfurls, we know that
even though

our time is smaller than a single now, an only once, that every
moment
in the miracle of mind and stars is so much more than enough.

(1998)

Five Complicities

for my mother, Edith Barrett Price

I.

She felt like a great exotic dry leaf in my arms.
I carried her up our steep back steps on the last Christmas Day
    of her life.
Homesick again, sleet in my bones, my mother's been dead for
    twenty-two years.
I savor her life, but I don't feel safe, *until*
she sets the softest trap to find me
in a place inside me I'd forgotten was still there,
a place where the past is never over and the future never runs out.
I see her, but cannot reach her. I hurry slowly
to catch up with her smile
down in the warmest ring of my heart
where I open out into the sky.

And there I feel her all around me in the night, her fathomless,
intimate cool hand on my brow, her smile
an epiphany of kind overlooking,
of vast forgiving beyond any ending.
Sipping champagne, kissing dark chocolates,
a Cheshire moon in winter skies, she hands me one
nylon stocking
heavy with candies, toy soldiers,
dreams of all kinds and surprises,
and welcomes me into her boudoir of stars, no brighter
than her eyes, an accomplice again
in homely joys, comfortably far and wise.

II.

What a Christmas it would be
if, as we fight off dying down the road,
with all our mysterious affections still in place,
we unaccountably succumb to feeling

quite gleefully safe, relieved, with a dire joy,
of all our worries, panics, paranoias,
of grim world history itself,
its infinite morgue of horrors,

relieved of the weight of everything,
the whole cosmos vanishing
like a film across our eyes,
everything, for us, all over. Gone.

Is that the same wild peace you felt
the morning you surprised us with your leaving?
Did you suddenly fall in love with your death,
was it like the scent of roses is to lovers,

or the sight of waists with red ribbons draped might be,
an inspiration to surrender up
the false safety of despair,
the voodoo of your nihilistic highs,

to live at last just edgewise for an instant more,
slipping through to happiness
under cover of darkness,
an accomplice in the sweet escape?

III.

Our lives are not problems we cannot solve.
Even making peace with the dread
tangles of child life, and all its sly oppressions,
is a craft to be learned. I remember my mother's
first frown at me when I wailed at tipping over
a cup of milk when I was five
and the redemption of her smile
and her advice, "Don't cry over spilt milk,"
she said, dropping a whole bottle of it
on the floor with a crashing splat.
What was *that*
miracle all about?

Is it that our friendliness with our flaws,
our unexpected patterns, our mad surprises,
teaches us that love's complicity
is everything we want with the night,
with the hundred billion stars in the Milky Way,
with the forces that conceived us
in the endless blossoming of light?
We want to be as intimate
with the source of all our wonder
as babbling toddlers are
bashfully stunned by being comprehended
when the source of all their pleasure

gives them what they want
because they asked for it.

IV.

When you died, it hurt so bad
the space you left became my anesthetic.
All that room's still left of you
and no one but you will know it.
I won't call it sobering. But it did
cause a mortal thrill in me
to think this Christmas, this most
intimate and simple fun, could be my last,
or one of the last four or five that I have,
not that I have any intuition that it will,
or any impending sense,

it's just that the math is working out that way.
These days are more and more
like an intimate, dreamy warmth
too sweet to ever end
ending right before my eyes.
That's why time's the great authority on joy;
and why we measure it.
Death caught you so fast.
No one wants to be a spendthrift
and forget to notice
the ride is always about to end.

V.

for Lou Andreas-Salomé

I've had this strange and dangerous urge
to confess my desire
to rehabilitate St. Nick.

So I confess it.
Just like the Christ baby is
all babies,

the infant spirit of the Golden Rule,
of you equal me and I equal you,
and not the infant Hitler of the Inquisition,

the sneering clerk inspecting all
the documents of the naughty and nice,
ol' St. Nick is not

the greedy giver of stock tics
in Profits R Us, stuffing our stockings
till our credit cards burst

with famine and the wealth of nations.
He's just a symbol for
everything friendly in our lives,

the happy comforter, the giver of surprises,
the imp of satisfaction with all hopes met,
the spirit of daddy warmth,

bay rum, starched shirts, and big hands
in the small of your back
soothing all distress

— an imp, however, nonetheless.
Santa's not a god.
Even our culture's happiest thought

couldn't make such sweet
justice, such friendly
pleasure the holy gifts they surely are.

(1999)

Five Mortal Pleasures

I. Perspective

Rising up from old mistrust,
there's nowhere to be anymore
but out beyond where we are, present
at the opening of the worlds,

star fathoming, spinning without a wobble,
far seeing who we really are:
blooming, painless, free; our hardships
as beautiful as turbulence seen

from the top of the sacred world; insight
opening so far around ourselves
we feel ourselves to be beyond our sight, so intimately
unknown all separation ends.

What joy to keep
just patiently rising.

II. Oasis

Seeing through the blues,
we've never lost a thing.
Veins of green along a canyon's edge,
verdant in seeps that flow through cracks

great cliffs have made so beans and corn
and squash can emerald through the desert:
This oasis of our days: What could be more
seriously down to the bone

than a green, wet truth when we're dying
of fathoming thirst? Ah, there it is:
Pure home. We've found it,
surprising us, around all corners, where hope

settles in to irritate despair.
Oases are everywhere.

III. Retreats

Waking up, we know there's nowhere to be
but safe — all friendship the veil of grace, even the terrible
friendship of the fathomless,
reminding us to trust

even the emptiest of spaces
all the way up to the full society of stars.
Hiding out, far into the farthest corners there, free
even from demands we should never really escape,

the mystery attracts us
like honest talk in old cafés
where conversation is the surf of truth
muffling the fear around us.

We are always just a thought away
from all safe harbors.

IV. Patience

Love is never amiss, the old poet said.
Bottoming out, even then the fulfillment is ahead.
It's always never too late, waiting with a will
to trust without knowing the purpose.

Fear is just a pack of lies. We have no choice
but to polish the mountain. Get out of the way. Patiently
calm down. Hope is never an illusion.
We're always on that sharp high wire

looping like a corkscrew
over the gorge of "rapture and despair."
Choosing the unknown, we feel the desire to breathe
is stronger than all

mad predicaments.
Yield to that desire.

V. Release

Having agreed, we changed our lives.
And still they died. Grieving scours,
scourges, scathes, it rakes us.
Gasping, we can't give up.

Loss begins for us at the very beginning.
We are all a massing of voids of the missing. This can't be said
any more than distance, space, deep time are said.
They are. Love is

never out of place.
Free falling back, we yield, released to be
gazed upon
by unknowable kindness.

Always the last true calling
is giving in to joy.

(2000)

Five Least Fallible Pleasures

Pleasure is not an infallible critical guide,
but it is the least fallible.

– W. H. Auden

I. This Is No Time to Be Vague

Purpose is a pleasure, the sly sage smiled.
This is no time to be vague. The whirlwind consumes
even the hands of the infants. We can't wait
for pain to get out of the way. Our whole world aches.
An old man screams, "What does peace mean?
I'm afraid I'm losing my self-respect."
There's no safe time to know your mind.
What's the purpose in waiting for the truth
and hearing a voice, too late, late at night,
say "I inwardly did nothing.
O Iscariot-like crime."*

What is the purpose? What do you mean?
Let's clean our minds and know what we know.
Kindness is a truth always worth trying.

*From Marianne Moore's poem "In Distrust of Merits."

II. Otherwise Can't Be

Sense is out of the question.
We're hated, we're loved
— no matter the explanation.
This happened, that didn't. That's it.
Nothing can be otherwise.
Acceptance is not resignation.
What sweet pleasure, then,
when resentment stops bawling.
What *does* peace mean?, the dying child will ask.
We can always pretend
to be effective,
though "certainly the means
must not defeat the end."*
Finally, we must answer.
Another question just won't do.
We will try "kindness," and try
being kind, and we'll think
it's not enough, somehow.
But the child will know.

*From Marianne Moore's poem "Values in Use."

III. "Hunt-Mad Hubert Startled into a Saint."*

It doesn't take much.
Vile catastrophe is more than enough
to shock us back to dangerous living.
Who doesn't, in her deepest heart,
want to help with all she has?
There is a best and a worst.
Conduct measures it.
The best overwhelms us every time
a person opens to another's need,
or yields in strength.
The best is there in the soft night of the mind,
when we feel with all we know that nothing can
go wrong, or is wrong, or ever will be wrong. And yet
the worst won't disappear.
The old woman pleads through her tears,
"What does peace mean?"
Her heart, filled up with the question,
is so patiently free, the truth
just baffles us with its secret joys.

*From Marianne Moore's poem "Saint Nicholas."

IV. Innocent Merriment

A whole biology of beautiful smiles,
winters calm as ravens shadowing through the pines;
dancing on cyclones we say
the bottomland truth to each other,
and Santa Claus finds his way to your beautiful heart
in the dark of the Christmas light parade.
We sleep the sleep of the blest
on the rim of the steepest decay.
"It's a pleasure to see so
much confusion."*
Merrily, merrily, merrily, merrily,
life is such a dream.
"What does peace mean?" he whispered,
remembering a hand on his wrist long ago
so warm, so deeply kind, he minds nothing anymore
of the crumbling life he leads.
As long as blood is the nectar of thought and the mind
blinks its constellations
there is more to a memory of love,
even of the slightest welcoming smile,
than to all the inconceivable loss of the world.
How practical love is.

*From Marianne Moore's poem "The Steeplejack."

V. The Satisfaction of Impossible Tasks

What *does* peace mean? It is not beyond us. There's just
so much debris to be carted off,
so much dust to be polished away. It's there, though,
just as we're still here under our wrinkles and luggage of fat.
"There's no unsuitable smile."*
Polishing a mountain's just too hard
when you want a definitive shine.
Peace and love are what they are,
and you have to be there, polishing, polishing. Devotion
is the question that answers can't resist.
Force ruins everything. Comets won't come when they're called.
Stars won't line up in a message and tell you what to do.
The one least fallible pleasure is, infallibly, just trust.
The impossible isn't a thing we can know.
It's unsuitable to think so.
"What does peace *mean*?" the tragic chorus pleads.
Every happy child can tell us with a smile.

(2001)

*From Marianne Moore's poem "Style."

A Few Rebellious Pleasures in the Reimagined Now

Being Calm

It's such a trick to play on power,
seeing through the feeble madness of the news.
What a comforting rebellion to be calm,
to refuse to goose step with the nearest fool.

Calm never lets us forget
how fearlessness is sweeter
than the dearest freedom granted by another.
Only one thing works, and it

can't really be spoken, except to say
that love will not deplete us, that generosity
is an ease so steely true, it overrides
blank cruelty every time, free as the calmness

of humility taking sides with each of us
who self-righteous stupidity has harmed.

Knowing What We Really Think

We are told the world is falling apart,
that nothing will ever be the same.
Don't believe it till you see it.

Sometimes humor is the only test,
an acid jest. Let's go see for ourselves
if the joke's on us:

our own way of thinking spreads out before us;
will we be the first to see its false horizons;
the first to report if the old maps are right,

or criminally charmed and wrong?
What a joke on force it is
to know our own minds. It makes us

like truth is, stronger than the strongest
and stronger than the worst.

Kindness

It catches everyone off guard.
It's an affront to fear.
It pushes the absurd smothering of joy
back out the door.
What a sweet dissent to refrain
from brutal truth.
Honesty for the sake of honor
has ruined everything it's touched.
Fulminate to yourself, but shut up for a while.
Break the rules. We were made for act of kindness.
All the rest — the suspicion, the nastiness, the greed —
is a bumbling, pitiful fraud,
and even indelible time
just wants to forget them.

What Matters

Us, each one of us, all of us, all humans
of any kind, no matter how we think,
or pray, or how we look or speak,
any single one of us who is wronged,

wounded, and maligned, deprived
of chance, good will and hope,
any single one of us forced by hate
to be less than uniquely who we are,

forced to say what we do not mean, forced
to demean ourselves just to make it through the day,
any one of us abused, disrespected and oppressed,
deserves a humble solidarity

from all the rest of us, every single one of us,
no matter who we are, or who we think we are.

(2002)

Five Gorgeous Losses

I. The Loss of a Few Stale Fears

Our dead pile up. Peace is snagged
like ducklings gobbled down by perch. Loss

consumes us, even as we come to lose
some of our dearest dreads. This is age's

consummation. Fear wears down to a darkening ember;
we're burned out on our horror of ghost sins

and failures moaning under the bed.
The joke we learn is that letting go

is the full and only meaning of control.
Even the loss of fear's mere dander

rings a bell: What a joy for a while
in the silence of the night, to open our minds and find

ourselves just rippling out beyond
the carrion smell of the myths of heaven and hell.

II. The Loss of Some Stupidity

Hope gets conned again. Suicide gulls the proud
with cruel applause for being pointless.
And even as we scream diatribes of grief

we feel in our selves the sweetest vanishing
of idiot delights, like spending life
as if it were money, calculating love

on a cost/benefit analysis, hating,
as fallen and debased, the whole
truth of the world that we know exists

with our body's infallible savvy.
Oh, go ahead, ask the hippo
to get off your foot. Wisdom's

too serious to be boring. It counsels
the painless safety to be absurd.

III. The Loss of a Little Ignorance

We think we know too much
about the look of death, about depression's
tangle of burnt roots. We even think
our ignorance knows no bounds and so
seems filled with knowing
what we cannot know at all.

It's wonderful to figure out, of course,
that the stars aren't holes in the sky, that everything
has to go somewhere, that motives
are so knotted none proves wholly true. It's more
wonderful to learn that knowledge is the road
to doubt and humble pie, to seeing mind itself

as a reassuring haze on the endless
deep surface of the Far-Beyond-Us.

IV. The Vanishing of Some Anger

Kindness drapes itself
with a more revealing fold than pain's
grim skirt of bones. Beauty and honesty
see each other home in the dark.

Shooting stars have shown us
death is not out to get us all alone.
How could we be rage-torn at bodies wilting
or leaves falling. It's ease we need

opposing cruelty that believes it's good.
The ease we have with fact
cancels anger as its own slow torture, dark
humiliation, comparing life

to solid dead abstraction. What a relief
to care so much we couldn't care less about judging.

V. The Absence of a Few Bad Habits

It's no different from removing
vestigial hooves from your heels,
or that pesky bony tail that pierces love seats.
It's a mundane metamorphosis,

the exotic revolution from the habit
of the normalcy of gloom. Even when friends
are falling all around us, we can still lose the guilt
of the automatic yes, the stunting caution

of the automatic no, the urge to force the truth
into a tiny hole not deep enough for a single fact.
Such wholesome heresies cheat grief, free us
from deforming lessons, wrong and old,

we can't defeat head on. They leave us illicitly
released and oh so gorgeously replete.

(2003)

Some Riffs of Merciful Defiance

... contraptions of the mind...
... Lady Philosophy says,
despair, dear children
is only folly's option...
nobody's pain is solved
without the wisdom
of intoxication... the play's the thing...
open the curtains
... Bacchus is so certain
he's the only consolation... let's not be too serious
... joy, it's so
mysterious; here's to a Christmas-morning life,
if you can tip
your inner sight
up to the light in your head just right; *Exuberance*
is beauty... inn-o-cent
merri-ment all the way...

... deepening peace in the jailhouse night
toss our torments down the drain
... the fury we suffer, skinned of the truth,
bone to a lie, give it up, she says,
it's snowing outside... Oooh, it's soooo
confusing, soooo amusing, swimming
in lava, Jack Frost nipping at your nose...
kindness is a property of atoms,
so are love, trees, pain, and stars...
junk the grand plans; help the old man
clean the snow off his car,
never say no to a stranger
looking for light in his head,
and yours...

... Scrooge, Scrooge, Scrooge be gone;
Santa loves the sugar in his cookies...
it's no mystery: deepening peace
will always be
a torment to the sour,
the grinding mind
will always find
a way to turn our sweetness
into a dour
privilege... let's not be
prematurely dead,
the light bulb out
in the icebox head...

... no, no, no...
No as a way of life? *Energy is
eternal delight.*
Rudolph with your nose so bright
let our No
guard Yes all night... kindness is
a new kind of sight... yes, yes, yes...
Ignore the preachers bored with light...
*He whose face
gives off no light
will never become a star...* yes, yes,
yes... Oooh, the hypocrites will so enjoy
punishing our joy... pun-ish-ing our jooooy;
ouch, ouch... oh botheration, oh
jubilation... *the sweet
soul of delight
can never be defiled...* in the warm,
free heart of the world at ease...

... Lady Philosophy comes to say,
take a big dump,
a big ego dump,
let it all go... and ho,
the bottomless pleasure
of being so
empty you'll surely know...

... come all ye lovers, let's give what we can...
the warm, free heart of the world
never closes, we just
can't find the seam, our lenses all fogged
like believing we're dreams... so rather than ache
unrequited, let's see them all before
their avalanche of years, as kids asleep,
full of their hopes, unbroken yet
on the rack of their fears...

... Mandela in his cell... Mandela in his cell...
old Blake in his garden singing to himself, *Joys
impregnate, sorrows
bring forth...*

... Oh, Rudolph with your nose sooooo bright
won't you guide my heart tonight?
... light, light, light... loving peace
and the world with all my might,
loving the world
        as the love
of my life...
oh badgers in the snow,
oh badgers in the snow,
oh badgers in the snow so white
can't we bunk with you tonight?

... don't crack, don't crack;
badgers in the snow so bright,
snarling through the dazzling night... they know
shame is just *pride's cloak*, they know... trust
is the only hope... enough is enough,
armor up... stay kind... but slice to the quick,
avoid, stall, infuriate, dance
out of the way, then strike... be good
at heart, but put the visor down, be open
and gentle without reservation, and sharp,
piercing, proficient... refuse, do not comply...

... the world is mad with love and fear
breathing the same pure air... don't crack, nothing
is more mysterious
than love you can't deny...
called to the good... God help you...
if your child's an outcast, so are you,
if anyone's in trouble, then so are you...
... and just the right smile at just
the right time
on anyone's kind face
can make
all veils of despair disappear, disappear,
all veils of despair disappear...

... breathe easy is the rule... do not
conform to hardship... old Eskimos go
outside to die, warming up to Nothing
by freezing in the night... the warm,
free heart of the world at ease,
deepening peace inside them...

... early snow across the mesas,
over the heavy breathing of the pines... it's all over
just ahead, swirling like a forest
in a hurricane of hail...

... star light, start bright, first star I see tonight,
wish I may, wish I might,
follow you throughout the night,
through the swamps of law and order oh so feral...
... oh, yes, let's not,
let's not comply;
if brutal means
soil perfect ends,
let's not comply... let's not
be a sewer of compromise...

breathe easy... deepening peace,
adore it like a fool
... let's drink a cup of kindness yet,
... *for everything that lives is holy...*
Who's to say who's the bigger fool?
... holy, holy, holy...
Who's to say who's the bigger fool.

(2004)

Quotations are from William Blake's *Marriage of Heaven and
Hell* with a nod to Boethius *in extremis* consoled by Philosophy.

Oracle News

The Oracle wasn't
all washed up at all.
But hope
is a real tough calling.

She used to knit scarves
to make her points,
warm with bromides, formerly wise,
still true:

> *Know Thy Self*
> *Moderation Wins*
> *You Must Change Your Life*
> *The Readiness Is All*

Few read them.
So she took to speaking
like so much graffiti.

> *God Is Home Sweet Home*
> she scribbled on boxcars along the way.

Then she made up some Christmas weather
out of the words of any old poet who came along.
One, denser than most, she heard pleading,
How *do* I change my life?
Is it true you can make
small adjustments
and everything fall into place,
like curing a limp
by good posture alone. Is that right?

> *Don't worry about what's right*
> she scrawled on fence posts.
> *It will come to you as strange advice*

It's not your fears
that matter, is it, the poet blurted,
not those over-excavated
looted digs, the archaeology of our terrors,
     not the bird flu,
     the terrorists, the hurricanes,
     cancers, tortures, humiliations, ice caps
     melting, poison gas, white phosphorous,
     vanishing oil, soiled water, war,
     not the demons of insult and disregard,
     the horror gods of paranoia?

     No. Why change? she sprayed on bridges.

What matters is doing good,
for goodness sake. Isn't it?
the poet wrote on his hand with a ball-point pen.
Let's not be lured
by the dope
of posthumous glory,
your whole life reduced
to merely the sound of your name.

     A joying we will go,
     a joying we will go
     she painted on railroad ties in Laramie, Wyoming.

Think of the relief you'd feel
if you could just stop
the drip, drip, drip
of cavernous complaint,
the inner whine, the low-grade fever
of sweaty carping, the gobbling,
eternal, dead-end critique, ragged
like the buzz of sirens in your ears,
the bells of St. Tintinnus stilled.

Ho, ho, ho,
a joying we will go,
hi ho the happy o
she scratched in fresh cement.

The oracle could feel her audience
turning away, straining to hear

the sweet, low wail of the damners,
and damned reformers and their giddy harps.

"How do I change my life?" the old poet pleaded.

Ho, ho, ho
a joying we will go;
I told you so, I told you so,
a joying sweet and slow
she doodled in Missoula.

Is that it?
the old poet scolded.
What about resentments,
cleaning them out
like blowing your nose
of night's debris,
that first release,
the oily dust of hurt,
incapacity, betrayal
sneezed up the chimney
with a "Happy Trails!"

Is that you, Santa Claus?
she penned on casts and braces all over the world.

Think of the fondest
dreams of ice.
Now there's some strange advice
she quipped on the sands of Waikiki.

When ego is replaced,
when acquiescence is erased,
what is
works out
into what
will be
without
using you
as manure,
the old poet doodled as if in a duel.

Dashing through the snow
knowing what you know,
hope is free to grow and grow
when it lets you go
she scribbled on bags of cat food.

A joying we will go,
a joying we will go,
good's in sight
and life is right
there's nothing more to know
she whispered into nurseries.

Rosa Parks,
now there's a hero.

Your mind's not to blame.
It wanders. Learn to ride it
she iced on scones in Nova Scotia.

But why is mind:
mind what I say,
and don't mind,
and never mind?

Paths exist, like mice trails
through the scrub and snow.

Don't find out what it's like
to be old without being wise.

>   *Take the numinous where you find it*
>   she wrote on the soles of sneakers.

We can't be told
but we know
that worry
has added
nothing
to nothing,
nothing!

>   *Be at home in happiness*
>   she jotted on the windshields of a billion cars.

Protect only
your openness.

>   *Can you tell*
>   *joy from success,*
>   *freedom from rebellion,*
>   *happiness from getting what you want?*
>   she chalked over playgrounds.

What's bliss?
she wrote on the clouds.

The supreme,
sweet, kindness
of choice
and the miracle
of the chance
that it matters.

Know nothing
is wrong
in a world that is
what it is
what it is
what it is
what it is.

Take sides.
Choose joy
the Oracle sighed across the windows of the world.

You must change your life.
Don't find out what it's like
to be old without being wise.

(2005)

Wild Joy
In the Dark Wood with Pan

> *Midway this life we're bound upon,*
> *I woke to find myself in a dark wood,*
> *where the right road was wholly lost and gone.*

– Dante, *Inferno*

Who if we cried would hear us
in the comic books of the gods?

Who would lead us with his dancing
through the melting woods?

Who would come to us, so rich in luck,
so pampered, daft, so gray around the muzzle?

Who would leap into the starry night,
whistling lullabies like comets croon the mysteries of light?

Only a dead god, loosed from dogma,
priests, dog mobs, and panics.

Never in the malls, or banks, or superstores
will the dead god dance us on our way.

Only in the turmoil of the inner forest,
only in the soundless turmoil of the stars.

The world's too hot and slick,
but Pan can dance upon it, Pan

can lead us to the wilderness
of joy in living right.

"Cry all you want," he sings, piping just ahead.
"I'm dead, a god, transformed into a love affair

with land and air, preposterous, beyond all care."
His advice to us, his map,

comes straight from our amazement
at having such a crush on this

wild god of panic, praise, and abject joy,
at falling so in holy love

with a dark beast of a world like this
ruled by chance and appetite beyond

our wildest scheming. "Follow me, follow me,
I will lead you to a Christmas tree,

will lead the way to innocence regained
and never once say anything

you must believe, or trust,
worry through, or comprehend."

***

Of Pan the flowery pastures sing,
Caves echo, and the fountains ring.
Sing then while he doth inspire;
For all the world is our Pan's choir.

     — Andrew Marvell

Let us go then, you and I,
through the doubt and fog

of Frankenstein's cruel science,
crying for a god to hear us

in the acid vats and salt crypts
of our poison reason.

Let us go through body codes,
laser bombs and nano holes,

crying for a god to lead us
through dusty words, narrow thoughts,

the killing smoke
rising from the engines

that keep our emails full
of ads for blue pills, stocks, and phony watches.

"Unreal city." The bosses overheard
second-hand that Pan was dead,

that the wild world was
a toy store, rendering plant, a huge

animal slaughtered over and over,
ground up and processed

into cars, and laptops, Formica table tops,
and they rejoiced in mint condition rolling

in their toilet tissue
greenback by the billions.

We grow old, we grow old,
our world's as firm as Kleenex in a gale.

No wonder we are drawn to gods
who seem more solid than the future,

being long gone, long ago, but here
not fossils, never dead,

imprints, though, and faintly true.
It's the Pan that matters,

not a goat legged little god
free as the evening air,

but all gods, Pan, everwise, everywhere,
taking our breath away, scaring us from death,

letting the worries of our days
teach us how to praise.

***

Come blessed Pan, whom rural haunts delight, come,
leaping agile, wandering, starry light... goatfooted,
horned,
from whom the world began; in endless dance and
melody divine,
in thee a refuge from our fears we find, those fears
peculiar to humankind.

— Orphic Hymn to Pan

Oh dark, dark, dark,
they've all gone into the dark,

lying and congested spaces,
false saints blowing on the sparks to blaze

their kindling dogma
into phantom flames, but Pan,

the residue of all,
the body of the hawk gods,

flaming bushes, lighting bolts,
flint butterflies, all tricksters

with their vulture smiles,
this all, this Pan,

the mighty forces of the world,
Santa Claus, and elves, and all,

at peace in comic relief,
answers all our seeking

in single moments
of suspended disbelief.

How can we complain?
Praise fears nothing.

"What you do
unto the least of my brethren,

you do unto..."
the rest of us.

Fighting the right fight,
surrendering to peace, opposing

what we know is wrong,
there's nothing anymore

to rail against, we agree
with divine graffiti when it says:

"never let joy
be one of your failures."

***

> *Dear Pan, master of grace*
> *in the Holy Mess we thrive in,*
> *teach us how to learn to be loved,*
> *... like beasts who finally trust enough...*
> *safe, calm, wild, fast, and unafraid.*
>
> – "Hymn to Pan," *Mythwaking*

Here we are in the middle way,
in the forest of our aging, hopes no longer

merely fears with fancy hairdos.
Can it be this randy, sleepy god,

is telling us to live
as if we are

unshakably
secure

in the pure
humor of the stars, the great

loving laugh that keeps the atoms
on their paths together, kind jokes

the journey and the glue of matter?
There are two gates of sleep,

the guiding poet saw,
one the glittering way

of false dreams in the world, the other
a footpath we can always walk upon

with holy images that are
plain

myth
bluff.

"Who I am
when I'm not afraid"

is the only gift
to ask for.

***

I sing of Pan, Nymph-leader... lord of winsome muses
when he pours forth the good-inspired siren-song...
and stepping nimbly to the melody leaps down
from the shadowy caves, moving his all-shape body,
fine dancer, fine of face, conspicuous with blond beard.

— Inscription from the Shrine of Ascepius
at Epidaurus

Where is the end of it,
the ponderous wailing?

We don't know much about gods,
but any can hear us as well as the next.

And all of them together
have big ears.

Let's let them tell us what to do.
Let's give in for a while, let go

and be the glorious memories
of long ago, of how

we have come to be
so happy.

We don't want to know what it's like
to be old without being wise.

Pan wakes us
to our daring.

All the gods want
from us

is the peace
to see right through them.

(2006)

With all thanks for Virgil, Eckhardt, Dante, Rilke, and Eliot.

Limbo's Angels

> *The goal is to make the ego as strong and*
> *as small as possible.*
>
> — C. G. Jung

Allons! The road is before us!
It is safe — I have tried it — my own feet have tried it well —
*be not detained.**

The broken world lay round about,
battered, poor, uneven, waiting for
an agile scout on the Feast of Stephen.
The mystery takes strange forms indeed,

Coyotes, Badgers, martyrs,
patrons of the widowed world,
the lands of hope uncharted.
But Wenceslas looked out one night

into ice fields breaking, and saw a poor man
come in sight and felt his soul awaking.
The world is cruel and kindness rare,

that is the fuel of reason;
we wait for life to lift us up
and make good luck more even.

Limbo life is crowded deep
with angels worn and waiting...

whereas
the mind

works
in possibilities,

the intuitions work
in actualities,

and what you
intuitively desire, that

is possible
to you.[†]

If we all were burrowed in
deep in intuition, we would know

we're free and clear now,
that nothing's in the way but us.

We don't need to wait
packed in limbo's dreading.

The bones of hope are beautiful in their bleakness
and Buddha and the Wise Men knew

a good star when they saw it.
It's all right here,

all innocent delight,
free of weak uncertainty.

No choking on the yes and no.
All we have to do is lose

our adorable thorn crowns,
our precious whaawhaas,

sentimental ouchies,
Freud's archaeology

all filled in, replaced
like a brachiopod

with beautiful fool's gold shine,
like end light glazing

crane wings from afar.
Ol' Nick, saint of all desiring,

wants us to have
only what we love, if

we give and give as though we knew
the frost is always cruel.

He asks us, in all
innocence,

what we want anymore,
now that the carcass

of our narcissism is
quite requited.

"Nothing
has mattered

but you,
and now you aren't enough.

What do you want?
You don't want to wake up at the end of your life

and find out you've been
a false friend to yourself."

... in the clearing of the winter gods
apples and fireflies adorn the pines.

... a free, plentiful world for all. That's the fight
and we are losing it. We don't know the magic of winning.

Victory is not forbidden,
failure is the trespass...

*A peculiar form of trespass is found among all clown [Koshare]
groups... Inverse to backward behavior or speech is, of all the
most characteristic trait... but is also dangerous...* ‡

Is that YOU
Yoda Koshare?

"Free be to
good is it.

Mask your off take," Ohhhhh.
Look out! All the snow

lay round about
your funny bones.

Screeching, wink laugh
I-don't-care

hilarity, and if I don't
it doesn't matter,

"matter doesn't it." Purging
strangulations

of serious intent:
Pull the wigs off,

unzip the flies in passing,
put salamanders down

pretty boy jeans,
it's the emetic that matters.

Laughter carries all.
It's the magic carpet.

Stand back, see
what you look like; oh no;

see how much fun it is
burlesquing freedom as if

to be free
was to be trapped

in freedom.
Break

into the clearing,
trespass,

love is only
forbidden

to those who can't
"self thy as

neighbor thy Love"
when the frost is even.

The boughs of the trees
are twisted
by many bafflings...[§]

San-ta Her-mes, cool Eartha croons,
comin' down the chimney al-right.

It doesn't matter what happens,
"matters it of

make we that only."
Whining in the car because

the games are boring, boring...
When a poor man comes in sight,

unbraid the knot you can't untie.
Yonder poor man who is he?

Trespass into happiness
for him, and you will truly see.

The kitchen door stays open, the lock
is always broken.

Speaking in tongues, "tongues in speaking"
say, "this whisper":

You, who are you
... What?

Can you hear
with your ego's beautiful ears

... What?...
the miniature sleigh

with the last right out
of pain and all its running fears?

You must love. A person, an island, an idea,
but it must be completely and with utter dedication.[1]

There's nothing that says we must
knuckle under to rich

expectations we know
are good for us but are

too good to be true
and so false we can't

be contained by them, unless
we say yes and give everything over

to being nicely better
than what's good for our souls.

Through the rude wind's wild lament
the joke's complete: we rarely

say the truth without
sounding falsely just too fancy: oh

just go
deep and clean

right's right
even if

it all seems wrong…
Fails my heart, I know not how…

Freud savored opposition.¶

Freud and his elves could tell
a rotten superego a thing or two.

"I heartily recommend the Gestapo to everyone,"
Freud wrote on his free pass out

between the Gestapo's slicking heels,
funny bone poking

the monster's literal eye.
You don't want to know what it's like

to be wise without being kind.
Even the monster in office needs

an egg not down his shorts.
When Koshares drive the sleigh they go

right to the seat of power, flushing
the occupant safe away.

There's no such thing
as kindness without restraint.

Put a thumb tack
under Idi Amin's

dada butt, or a briefcase
blast near Hitler's chair,

or bump off Caesar
and what do you get

bippiti boppiti boom.
Dada will dada you.

You don't want to know what it's like
to blow yourself up with your scruples.

Don't give
anything up

or away
to anyone

who says
trust me.

I know.
Trust me

or I won't
trust you.

It is
the fight.

"In opposition
is true friendship."

"What is
is perfectly what is."

You don't want to know what it's like
to have wasted your own

irreplaceable life
in the dungeons

of your lazy,
old tired sorrows,

to be so trapped
in look-alike frauds

that life has to be right
for you to be happy.

*When he turned fifty, his country was obliterated, his family
erased. He hid his traces by dwelling in the mountains... Casting
his mind back to a time twenty years before, it all seemed as if the
world had been cut adrift.*[◊]

A vein of dust
runs through us all,

sifting uselessness all over.
Our true, old purity's intact, we find,

when we dust it slowly. It's ever hopeful
we'll catch up, and clean it merrily before

the sour ashes of our spent despair
sand blasts flat our old true beaming,

the baby joy, the dream of life
we know is not our dreaming,

the lightning marvel of the sense we feel
that "everything that is

is holy" for a reason.
What better way to spend your days

than praising what you've always known,
and never known by reason?

(2007)

*Walt Whitman, "Song of the Open Road"
†D. H. Lawrence
‡Elsie Clews Parsons, *Pueblo Indian Religion*
§H. D., "Hermes of the Ways"
ǀBryher quoting H. D. in *The Heart to Artemis*
¶Mark Edmundson, *The Death of Sigmund Freud*
◊from the Notebooks of Zhang Dai, ca. 1644

A Gift Has No End
A Masque for Christmas

Stage Directions: As usual, everyone is talking all at once. The scene is a cold night in high moonlight. Bare stage. People, myths, and choral beings are milling about, dressed eccentrically, waiting for something to happen. Some in the crowd might be wise. It's hard to tell through the din.

Chorus:
>Pains condense,
>rot out thinner values.
>No pain is worth
>the pain of fear.
>The miracle cure
>is not minding.
>Give attention
>to something else.
>Attend to indirection.
>Luck is open hearted.

Caliban Jr.:
>The foibles of joy mount up.
>Will the shoelace of our worry
>trip us up on the stairs,
>going down to the basement
>of auto suggestion?
>Will we lie there
>hypnotized
>affirming only
>a mumble?

Hermes:
>Vanished panics are so sweet.
>Pines' thick fur
>on the wild body of the mountain,

smooth as hawk glide, shadowless
and pure between the branches,
patches of sky in storm clouds,
the lake ripples its skin
like horse hide shivering off some flies.

Chorus:

Solipsists, subside.
Fixation chokes the flow.
The poodle doesn't know you.
In a golden wig
approach the bull.
Your dark refusals
deafen no one.
Childhood withers,
good deeds
are certified stale,
dark thoughts
melt the thinker
when he thinks.
Fix not. Just,
and we say just,
just turn, turn away,
turn around,
turn and leave.
The fix is off.
Go nowhere near.

Anti-Chorus:

Where's the manger?
Where's the star?
Was the paranoid reporting?
Was rumor cruel?
Oh god I'm tired.
Where's the fun?

Mom's abed full make-up on,
she gave her ermine coat
to orphans out of spite,
god bless her; she fills her nylon
with oranges and toys,
a long sausage of matchless joys.

Joseph:

I tell you. I know what happened.
Nothing. Really nothing.
More chaff, please, more chaff.
A little more. The grinding
finds its comfort
in always a little more.

Mary:

He's right. But he's out of his mind.
He doesn't know what he's saying.
He's right, though.

The Baby:

Want to make me laugh?
The foibles of joy confuse me.
Don't confuse me
with the Big Baby.
Gimme, gimme.
Come on.
Yes, innocence is greedy
for everything and everything else.
Experience is not
corruption. Innocence is not
above it all.

Wise Old Me:

Disentangle. See.

Scared Old Me:
　　I tripped
　　on insight,
　　fell right through.
　　It's the wrong leg,
　　the wrong leg,
　　the flight of the bumble bee...
　　is the eye of the needle
　　too small?

Wise Old Me:
　　Be real.

Scared Old Me:
　　Yeah, right.

Chorus:
　　If you don't mind,
　　or at least pretend,
　　nothing spooks
　　horses racing,
　　not even a napkin
　　blowing across the scrub
　　of thought, magnified
　　in the horse's eye.

Mary:
　　Why me just doesn't matter much
　　when the angel clears its throat
　　and continues. You have been so honored.
　　You can't do anything
　　about it. That's grace for ya.
　　How do you not mind that?

Joseph:
> Okay. So I'm a poor substitute.
> So, I don't mind really.
> Please...

Wise Old Me:
> I'll just look away.
> I don't want to see.
> I don't want to know.
> I don't. I can care
> without knowing exactly.

Chorus:
> Solipsists! Lo
> unto you this day is hatched
> a plot to have your words
> cover you like an elephant trap
> is covered with leaves.
> Not minding
> has nothing to do
> with not caring,
> not wanting to help.
> Pain prevents the gift.
> Don't mind
> the pain, and the gift
> can never be stopped.

Anti-Chorus:
> Oh, please. Let's not talk
> of funny pants.
> The only plots that count
> are those that mean
> we're safe asleep.

Chorus:
> Retrieve yourself.
> That's Plato for you:
> All or nothing,
> and not quite enough.
> Do and don't do as you're told.

Hermes:
> You don't have to smile when you say those words.
> Just think of what would happen
> if you could
> say no.

Mary:
> Don't go there.

Joseph:
> Don't confuse me with the one
> who thought he hadn't.
> I'm just a guy who can't say no.

Wise Old Me:
> Oh, so this isn't
> what I thought?

Chorus:
> Solipsists,
> just give a bit,
> just open up,
> dark decisions
> have no empty pockets.
> Look the other way
> when fear catches your throat.
> Minding makes the difference.
> A gift never ends.

The beggar and the book man
so beloved: Both are gone.
You don't have to mind
to care.
A gift never ends.

Badger:

Anyone need a room for the night?
Assorted pixies
came to lunch
on sticky buns and bacon;
the den was warm
and snakey dogs
and bigger bears
couldn't snag us
through the roots.
So safe we were,
we raised our pinkies
with our tea.
We told the secret stories
of the lives we would have lived.
And each of us wore
quilted and embroidered bibs.
We shook off fear
like horse hide twitching flies.

Wise Old Me:

Did you get any presents?

Badger:

Takers and givers. That's
our world. Down here
all we are is safe. The Angel
always likes her tea with us.
She brings her star in a beautiful down box,

duck down, pheasant, swan.
And then the star is born!
There's no business like show business.

Wise Old Me:
Pretending
and not minding
are in the same play
we're all in.

Pan:
The vast mystery
of being happy:
the trust of fun
is never empty.
The rain that Eve
in '46, an ocean's hymn
streets slick with stars,
a bright warm store
full of impossible delights,
your hand in your father's
as he studies the shelves
to give you a gift
to please your mother.

Chorus:
Too big a crowd. Back up.
We're singing.
"... shadowless and pure
between the trees, like patches
of sky in storm clouds,
like a lake ripples its skin,
like horse hide shivering off some flies."

Anti-Chorus:
>   What an odd refrain.
>   Come close,
>   we don't exist, all of us
>   have no voice at all,
>   just presence.

The Baby:
>   Am I going to grow up
>   to be
>   Jesús
>   García*
>   with his train on fire
>   full of dynamite,
>   the blast a light
>   at the end of all tunnels in the dark?

Hermes:
>   I'll be on the train.
>   I won't jump off.
>   Luck is openhearted.

Pan:
>   Man, oh man
>   do I ever want
>   to take a nap.

Chorus:
>   Try too hard to be noble
>   and you end up a priestly scrooge.
>   Look over there, how he
>   turns his back on joy.
>   How he sticks up his nose,
>   how he really wants those
>   pantsuits in the window.

Anti-Chorus:
> Check your libretto.

Chorus:
> No. Pantsuits, it says.
> See how he covets the world
> to conform to his fears,
> conform to his needs,
> conform to his bitchy whims
> of perfection, his silage
> of limitations and diminishments.
> S. Vignette has said,
> "Apocalypse is a by-product
> of vanity."

Anti-Chorus:
> The old gate we've carried
> to every passage, it never
> fails to open. It's so easy to mistake
> obsession with prudence.

Hermes:
> Luck is openhearted.

Joseph:
> There's nothing wrong.
> I've asked and now
> I understand. My place
> is at the head
> of the Mad Hatter's table,
> not because I suffer
> delusions of grandeur
> but because I know
> what the Garcías
> are going to feel

when the generous
heart of their Jesús explodes
and the town
not far away
is saved.

Chorus:

One wish for all, one wish for all.
He didn't mind.

Caliban, Jr.:

"Question not
invisible forces.
Magic will happen,"
Ralph Waldo was made to say.
The shepherds were "midnight ramblers."

Chorus:

Who has the Parables?

Hermes:

He turned the old man away,
he turned the old, toothless man away,
he rationalized he didn't have the teeth to eat with
anyway. He was in a hurry.
He hit a dog, and moved on. His identity
was stolen by a lookalike;
it's not me; no one would believe him.
He saw his unpublished book
on the shelf under another name.
The police were looking for a madman,
he fit the bill. And when he tried to convince them
they concluded he stole the lookalike's identity
and sent him to jail wailing.
He did go mad. And everyone refused him water.

Joseph:

He wrote and wrote.
He never pulled his punches.
He was honest to the core.
He was totally hateful
and a drop of poison
wherever he went. And yet
he was lionized, like dimwit leaders
are lionized in times of trouble,
he was lionized and the children
adored him. The priests made him
into a flawless teller of flawless truth.
When the children finally found out
from him that Santa Claus wasn't real,
they fell to the ground in wanton grief,
and found they were weeping in Santa's beard.

Chorus:

Any more?
You'll have to shout.

Badger:

I dug the old lady out,
up through the brain jail floor.
She slipped right through the hole.
The shrinks couldn't shrink fast enough
to catch her. She was free,
and gave the little boy all that he needed:
one person to hear what he said.
A gift never ends.
There really is
nothing but beauty,
if you don't mind
to give.

Anti-Chorus:
>Now wait a minute.

Pan:
>What's more fun
>than shaking up the world?
>Takers don't
>know how to receive.
>Luck is openhearted.

Stage Directions: The lights dim. All turn, facing the audience. The din ceases and in one voice they sing.

All:
>And what to our wondering hopes did appear
>but a long winter's nap with nothing to fear.
>The back door bolted, the front door locked
>our brains settled down, our thoughts were unblocked.
>We dreamed what we loved: the desperate were saved,
>the ruthless long gone: joy has no age.
>Whatever we want, we give it first hand;
>our attention will never turn into sand.
>Pretend, pretend, the gift has no end.
>Pretend not to mind, and it won't be pretend.

(2008)

---

* Jesús García was born in 1881 to working-class parents in Nacozari, Mexico. He worked his way up from water boy to engineer of a steam locomotive hauling copper ore from a Phelps Dodge mine and taking workers, supplies, and explosives back to the mine. In 1907, when García was 25, the dynamite boxes on his train caught fire near a powder magazine which held another

500 tons of dynamite. Without hesitation, he raised the steam in his engine and headed for open country, ordering his crew to jump. In half a mile the dynamite exploded. The town and its people were saved. Jesús was a cheerful and openhearted man who lived by the Mexican adage *a lo dado no se le da fin,* a gift has no end.

Five Ways Home

I. The Chaco Way

Giving his life
its head, mind riding
thermals
over the cliffs
where nothing ever goes wrong,
the perfectly
what is
detects him
like raven's shadow
fast across a ridge.
Fear thins out.
Nacre skin, fossil
Aphrodite's perfect
blush appears
so touchable her knees
smooth into stone,
and he hears himself say
"I have no way of knowing.
I have no doubt.
Light might know. My body might.
I'm just feeling my way around in my brain
looking for what's in my madness
for flying through rock,
in badgers dreaming of saying no,
in the flood off the cliffs
that never came.
Though I do know faultlessly
that as keys open locks
lives open vaults of the given
and everything is
no longer missing
at last."

II. Paris Satori

Altered states
are what we're made of.
When pain turned itself
into his body,
the mercurial became
the fundamental.
The state of himself
confounded him.
He startled who he was
with who he is:
On the road to the Luxembourg Gardens
in a back street breeze on a Paris morning,
he was stooped as a fairytale villain,
back full of ache and acid.
He walked through the gate
into the shade of the Chestnut arcade
and straightened out like a willow bough
snapping free from river mud moving on,
pain ignoring him
as he tall-walked with the children
around the sailboat pond.
An altered state
had loosed him.
It happened. His body knew it. How
was beyond him. Some days still
he returns to the nerves of Paris
like a glance at Venus
over his shoulder, and feels clean
through the pain of the world and out
the other side of his body.

III. Free on Fenton Lake

Right behind the mirror,
right behind the tinnitus
of monologues, the ruins of twilights
across a life, right behind
is the pause that opens
everything, a window of always,
like stepping out
onto a lake, walking
on frozen water,
on water in a different state,
like their minds
were altered to become the dusk,
breathing in and breathing out
on little chairs
on solid water
in the center of the lake,
the fishermen around
wondering if they'll pull
whole fish through the ice
without a hole,
silent ice shamans. No
fish, ice cutters lose
their focus on them fast,
while theirs has opened
to the single moment
through which the whole
cosmos fills
their breathing,
trusted as the ice,
as the un-
questioned next
whole
breath.

IV. Thanksgiving on the Duranes Lateral

Turkey in the oven,
he counts his blessings on the ditch.
Night soil keeps no history. Scars
and vandal pocks
reduce to blessed events. "Shit
floats," alimentary, easy
goes it. The walk's too full
for pain. He never forgets
who saved his life,
who graced him
with the luck of kindness, the stress
of torments slipping out
into his life, teaching him how to dance
on boulders of ice.
Most all of them
time has misplaced.
He imagines
all the nows with them,
not what he wanted to happen, but what did,
the bounty in the paradox.
And he feels obstructions passing, his luck
still with him, the whole
pantheon of his life, the perfect
myth forms who formed him,
the fortune of fate, still strong
in legs that still
know how to walk
under a heart that still
knows how to praise.

V. The Christmas Way

He knew that places are states of mind.
Snow moon along the river,
tidal light shadowing sleep, all
so far from now
marvels of comfort can still
save hope from the hard
devils of the heartless.
Thoughts, he argued, foreshadow
what comes to be.
When he turned so furious
at the world he saw
no way out for himself,
no sanity, no honor,
then there was only
one solution:
to be
what he needed:
The peace of the starry cold
in the weathered barn long ago,
a shrine
to what matters,
where he first felt he was known
as he really is
and he heard the defiant
old woman tell him true as waves
his freedom to this day:
"Give what you need.
Give what you need."

(2009)

Hanging On by Letting Go

Memories of the great gifts, the geode midnights:
    the universe a cave of stars

ablaze with Eros, photosynthesis, the unimaginable
    delight of light, of human warmth of any kind,

of body peace, dawn thrill, sweet death
    when you need it.

Miracles of kindness, of someone knowing
    what you need to hear

and saying it for nothing,
    knowing what you need to have

and opening the way for you to have it
    without a fearsome price,

taking fears apart for someone young
    and handing her a free day

with nothing left to do but live all out,
    safe and free as finding by surprise

crane-haven woodlands out of sight,
    like lovers' grace, a truth with no opposite,

getting what you want in a world that doesn't want you.
    Such joys, we know, are once only,

one after one after one. If you have them
    as you have a breath, if you are them,

you are them forever.
    All past is infinite in us

like reality is in itself
     always there, remembered or not,

perceived or not. What was
     is who we are.

The past has no past
     when it was not. For us,

it is always the hanging on,
     one now after another, letting go

of all precarious terrors,
     dark fogs of dread,

cutting the puppet strings of ancient,
     carping habits.

Each moment lost to a fierce supposing
     is a death of now,

imagination running off with you
     when you are meant to be

in complete control,
     if you only knew it,

free to make an inner world,
     any world you please — a badger's lair

with a full larder and a good library, a pharaoh's
     forbidden flower paradise out our back door,

a poet's den of the wonders of love lost
     and found — better some delusions

than the phony absolutes of fear.
     Every time we look ahead through

frames of expectation,
     what is

evaporates before it can become us. Death is an empty pool
     in which to gaze and walk away.

Get over death.
     The craft of surviving through to the end

is an acrobat's trick of will
     — falling just doesn't work,

isn't worth the thrill.
     Stay in the air, letting go, then catching on

all the way to the ground on your feet;
     it's far better than a fatal thud.

Skywriting hope with your body,
     words just come for you to live by

when you ask for help.
     What do I do now?

Don't mind.
Be glad.
Be free.
No stress now.

The answers came
     like acrobats without a net

— the law of *not minding* is not
      that troubles don't matter,

it's just that they are
      forgettable

before they're even remembered
      like most blemishes of pain, most flat days.

The glad, free mind talks them away.
      They have nothing to say but sly depression anyway.

Not minding is not ignoring, or denying:
      it is not bothering to object because

there is more, so much more than mere objection
      to be had. The hope of *being glad*

is to see, and be, the totality of what's
      not wrong,

all that's left when what you've minded not
      is no longer on your mind.

That kind gladness is forever ready;
      it's only misplaced for as long as you forget

the acrobat's best trick:
      even flying through the air with the greatest of ease

thanks always works on a slippery trapeze.
      The truth of *being free*

is to peel off the impulse to predict. All scripts
      are hot molasses, simmering fly traps,

tar baby supposings. Hang on to the air,
    let go, free fall, you'll catch yourself.

The gift of *no stress now*
    is being always one now at a time,

not denying history or pretending fate,
    not living in the never never of what is not,

but in all
    that is. That

is the peace that passes as the only solace.
    We know that every safety, each pleasure, all delight

passes on from the never yet
    into the always was, just as every horror does.

What a gift that great disappearance is,
    not unlike humor

as a cosmic fact is — cats with long toes
    pawing Rachmaninoff piano concertos,

dancers with magic hair entwined like Castro's
    vociferous beard with Einstein's tangoing mop,

moral time warps where Mighty Mouse is offered
    Hitler's hair cream and declines.

Oh the genius of the good hand on the back,
    the call when we think no call will come,

the gift that starts the gift you are
    moving into being, they are all as much

of what the cosmos is
        as gravity is. Kindness is not

anomalous. It is the climate of compassion,
        the prevailing weather

of the brunt of humankind
        that heals what sores it finds,

that would solve its way through every
        dark, unfathomable disaster of the mind.

It knows what the blue heron means
        flying with you as you drive, window high,

barely off the ground, not 20 feet away,
        staying with you, low enough

for you to feel its wings, improbable as you
        leaping up and flying, the heron

eyeing you from the corner of your eye
        as if it saw *you*

as a miracle. Aren't you glad you weren't
        off minding tomorrow,

that you'd let go
        of everything that's wrong,

so a wild, unlikely artifact of chance,
        effortless as lucent stone

yielding to the light, could be for you so free
        as to be quite holy

as the trust you find
    offering your life

to what you feel is right
    and true,

and letting go
    so it can heal you?

(2010)

Feral Pleasures
(Et in Arcadia Ego)

> *If others examined themselves, attentively, as*
> *I do, they would find themselves, as I do, full*
> *of inanity and nonsense. Get rid of it I cannot*
> *without getting rid of myself. We are all steeped*
> *in it, one as much as another, but those who are*
> *aware of it are a little better off — though I don't*
> *know.*
>
>   – Montaigne

> *Et in Arcadia Ego (Even in Arcadia, I).*
>
>   – Virgil, et al.

[Arcadia: a free, feral place and state of mind,
innocent of the tyranny of hierarchy, conformity,
and cruel habit.]

Et in Arcadia Ego: those wild, pure breaths of childhood,
alone on your bike, troubles behind you;
tide pools and sea anemones,
a soda shop with steamed windows,
a great street of pines in the rain, all ahead:
the first time you heard the inner voice
and knew
it did not
come from you.

We are there again
even when we're not

— in Pan's
playground —

even here
even now.

We can
be as happy

as we want,
especially

in idyllic
nowheres where

the mad
now of the world

is wallpaper
peeling off,

dangerous
slightly, but then

death will be
seduced by you

whatever you do.
Nowhere can be

a better place.
It's never now.

It's always now.
A refuge is always

awaiting our attention
inside us.

If we can
conceive of it,

we can
partake of it.

Et in Arcadia Ego: The Alchemy of Innocence
never fails; paradise is still in the worst and the slightest;
you're in your parents' bed with a cold, the big bed,
and in on a tray comes hot chocolate and comic books
rolled and tied with ribbons; Jemez river snow fields
hidden in the pines, water mesmerizing over rocks.

When I'm away,
I'm always here,

in these idylls,
on these shores

where the Emptiness says
nothing is lost,

though everything is
about loss,

lost but never
abandoned,

heaven on Earth
always going,

always gone, always
present, never

vanished,
never seen again,

always elsewhere,
always here.

It is so simple and so
ungraspable —

it is true
that mere words

can make
a world real,

like a smile can
change a body's chemistry.

Et in Arcadia Ego: Where was that Christmas tree
alight in the woods, not on fire with flame, but on fire
*   with delight?*
Where was that saint of the beautiful rough smile,
hands hard as firewood, her laughter a chorus of light?

Badger and Ratty and Mole
about to bed down in a larder

— some call them vermin.
Badger is mean; Ratty dirty;

Mole a garden vandal;
but in mindland, the alchemy

of Innocence rescues us
from the tacky

inquisitions of the literal,
the poisoned cotton candy

of the fantasies of hate,
and lets them fall

on a pile of ants and manure,
uneatable.

How may we elude
vile allusions?

How may hope
grow in us again

like weeds
in concrete?

Can we let
the great gifts

lift us through
the fumes and gore,

and set us down
on a chill morning

in a warm kitchen
to the side, behind

bleak woods, where thoughts
thaw at the hearth

of an altered mind
joy dancing

through a perfect
world, no different

from the world right now
— if illusion is

the substance we are made of?
Might ecstatic thought,

might comfort and joy,
override cruel history

for days at a time,
even its hidden stories,

the ones we know nothing about
but feel in our breath like scars?

Et in Arcadia Ego: The stranger in the parking lot
wheeling his girl in a stroller, using her for bait to get
what they both need more than imagery; it's not a con
to get a bite to eat, not undignified to find a way
not to die; and you're the one, by accident, who happens
by, graced, for a moment, with a free open mind
and a buck or two to spare.

The presents all pile up,
lifetimes of openings,

thought windows airing out
the body of its sorrows,

opening on to mornings
stretching into libraries

of time, horizon upon horizon.
For some, such mornings

never come, childhood
a slow starvation, slave labor,

winter-lost in sulfurous dark woods
— but even these heroes

who luck never blessed
with warmth, even they

remember in the depth of yearning
how much the day adores

our attention, like the greatest gifts,
the ones that caught us by surprise,

the gifts never asked for,
the ones that changed our lives.

Et in Arcadia Ego: Christmas morning on my mother's bed
two years after the war, her nylon stockings filled
with oranges, apples, walnuts, and toys,
thumbing her nose at want and fear, at cruelty
and the long suppression of her joy by the knowledge
of the suffering of others.

These are the dreams of safe people
with no enemy yet,

with warmth and food enough to fantasize
the universe conceives

of happy spirits too,
consoled in dreamy winter nocturnes,

ballets of lullabies, freed
by all the care that's given

with a pure desire
to give.

Such a Catalogue of Kindnesses:
A forgiveness you didn't deserve;

an understanding you hadn't earned;
luck's blessing blindsiding your terrors:

The time a stranger pulled you up
by the arm from a shallow

shoreline riptide turning you
upside down, close to all but dead,

then standing upright, redeemed
in the twilight on the sand; or when

your child looks into your eyes,
then puts his arms around your shoulder;

or the day, cleaning up a mess
of carelessness and malice,

we find those groves of light,
woven in crowns

around everyone's mind,
shining to reveal

that wild poise
we have all misplaced,

from time to time,
and found again

just when we had to find it, that great
kindness of the absent gods,

and we come upon
the caroling of morning,

see our face in another's face
that feels the same, when you see it,

as the delight of one
in the peace of many.

Et in Arcadia Ego: The time you tossed a rock to see
how far you could toss a rock and it hit a car because
you couldn't toss it far enough, and the driver,
charging up the hill after your father, shouting
that black-haired kid in a red shirt and white pants
shot at his car with a gun, and you, there with ogre dad,
blond, wearing a white tee shirt and blue jeans
— knowing the boulder just missed you — that's a feeling,
a utopia of chance, so private, so indelible, it never forgets you.

The world of our hopes
is always in us;

we can always
be to ourselves

who we want to be,
we are in charge

of our own definition
of who we are.

Bad spots abound.
"Slide over this world

a bit lightly." We are
the stories we invent:

fantasies mean us
more than we intend.

The play's the thing.
Et in Arcadia Ego.

Where we are
is where we think

we are. We have all
the time we want

anytime we want it.
Innocence is

an idea. Ideas
are thoughts.

Thoughts are real.
Is anything not

what we think of it?
Just think of it!

The feral mind
knows no bounds.

Oh, do not
tame it.

(2011)

Secret Victories
[What's left of a lost manuscript of Lucretius]

O pitiable minds of men, O blind intelligences!
In what gloom of life, in how great peril is passed
all your span of time! not to see that all nature barks for is this,
that pain be removed away out of the body, and that the mind,
kept away from care and fear, enjoy a feeling of delight!

[What follows is a loose and fanciful translation of
mental fragments once scattered and now gathered
and placed for Sapphic effect in six parts in keeping
with the method of Lucretius. Italic epigraphs are
from Lucretius, Epicurus, and the Lesser Epicurus.]

I. How It Is

We can be as happy as we want.

Oh Venus, if you will, please send a philosophic thrill
running like a bolt of hope right through us...

In the Garden of Epicurus the Chorus sang
the first word of Logos — Glad...

glad in service... glad in health,
glad the first condition... glad,

... which conquers... even pain...
in the refuge of our thoughts...

... All persuasions have an opposite
and exist along a spectrum... But

kindness is not a proposition.
It is a joy...

self-evident as its opposite...
(as) the dark chances and perfect follies

that hound us all our lives.
... How laughable for us to cause

our own... shame and misery...
when the road outside is full of monsters...

It is in the nature of things
for us to be abandoned and in charge

of our own delight and failings... but...
and yet... grace *is* all... not laughable at all

for failure to prevail
when all it does is lose.

... (It is) the science of the secret life
... the geode life resplendent within itself...

to comprehend... peace of mind...
and seek it avidly.

All understandings are partial;
the Absolute is beyond us.

(I, Lucretius, the invisible Roman
with no life in history, but my books,

once argued otherwise. Matter is
what matters; it is first;

what is not matter
has emerged from it, I said.)

... don't mind... life is more than matter;
even I, the Epicure, can't resist the excess... starry magic

... of the holiest
holiness of life... Venus Aphrodite Eros

... Love,
the binder and joiner of all,

the shimmering pleasure no one
can refuse or refute...

How it works (is this)
... for us... mood is matter,

outlook is
determining as atoms.

All is chance and choice,
... no plan... we can know...

Mind is gravity
around which love

and chances swerve. That's why
"Despair is no good"

... (it's) as if our fears and bleak surmises were
actually not

a species of delusion...
The world forever seems

on its last legs...
children notice it

and despair until
they see...

adding pain
to pain is not

a child's game...
and repair to the tree house

for their fantasies of hope
where Harry, Peter, Bilbo,

Santa, Flash and Tarzan
in their glory roam

in refuge and high solace and seclusion...
Adults forget. We live

in cramped obscurity...
with sinister gaffes and guffaws...

the geode cracked...
rotting black... but No!...

No! scrub the mess,
polish mountains,

shine... Pleasure
has such shapely wings.

II. Thinking Makes It So

What is blessed and indestructible
has no troubles, nor does it give trouble to anyone else.

It is laughable to think
the cosmos cares enough

to spend its time
tormenting us to make us better

... and yet... we are fools,
foul narcissists... broken mirrors

mock us everywhere...
... "Dispositions of the mind,

like limbs of the body, acquire strength
by exercise"... Exercise Doubt. It will set you free...

When you doubt the premises that seem god given
... (that) suffering in last place (let's say)

is part of a sacred order... hierarchy...
be free of it... Premises matter

more than matter does to us.
Beasts... like us evolve

by thinking. Humane
logic in action

is the Golden
Fleece... to change the premises

of our bondage...
Thinking works

an alchemy... we see
the world as we say it.

What you say you are
you are to yourself... idiot...

hypocrite... too humbled
to be wise.

III. Death Is Nothing

Of the things which wisdom provides
for the blessedness of one's whole life, by far
the greatest is the possession of friendship.

... The world stage has
one trap door

that moves
and opens randomly,

... a lethal rendezvous, catching everyone, some
with many tremendous

near misses... anywhere we happen to be
... at least we fall into a vacancy...

So Death is nothing
we can know...

(but) friendship (is)
everything... that matters...

Born into history...
as we are, knowing nothing of what

once was but hearsay, and nothing of
what might be but rumor and panic and conspiracy,

... We stay who we are all our lives
while changing everything

about ourselves except
our secret core,

which only friends detect
through the lens of attentive time

... the gift of loyalty...
which turns... existence back into itself

so that what we do
becomes exactly who we are.

And then we aren't.
We vanish. And the world

vanishes before our eyes
because our eyes

are gone. That is all we sense.
And that is all our senses tell us.

... And in this world of fictions
we are mere extras...

without the coffee cups,
the booths, the kitchen tables

and the trusted...
across from us... only... only

with our forgiveness
are we forgiven.

IV. The Gifts

No pleasure is a bad thing in itself.
But the things which produce certain pleasures
bring trouble many times greater than you'd like.

We are made for gladness.
... it is laughable to suppose

one wild idea... one dogma
is true alone... and none else are.

Joy, itself, is a mystery of matter
... not a myth...

Venus is... a mystery more
than metaphor...

We are made of the same stuff...
as the sum...

total of the measureless...
... this is why...

in a world where pain
defines... and seems an infinite,

some of us, in secret
overcome it... to live in gladness...

by simply giving our attention
to everything else that doesn't hurt.

... That's the secret victory
we share and cannot say

... except through sympathy... which is
the way...

V. Most Pleasure

The removal of all feeling of pain
is the limit of the magnitude of pleasure.

It is laughable to say
the universe is

what it is, and not say (it is)
what it can be, too...

fact and potential.
(And we are)... the same;

our bodies know
... delight is

finer than
the longest

traditions...
of the the miserable...

delight
in communion with...

mysteries of kindness
we can only praise...

It is impossible to live pleasantly
without living prudently, honorably,
and justly and impossible to live
prudently, honorably, and justly
without living pleasantly.

VI. The Terrible Is Easy

Life is one long struggle in the dark
until we understand the light
at the end of the tunnel
is all... insight...

as warm as the winter music
of the cranes...

It is laughable to think
we are made to suffer,

to merely survive
until our genes have had their way, or...

to serve as slaves to the whims of others.
Ask us and we will tell you... all of us...

no, we were made for meaning and delight...
... It is in the nature

of the way of logic
that we are not

here for what we must avoid,
but here for what we always want

and seek... what we are made for
... (as) badgers are made for digging and holing up.

Most pleasure with
the least pain...

a calculus
for every action,

every decision,
every time... deliberating

can set us sane
in the mad pit

of our wants and compulsions... and so...
don't mind, be glad,

... trust change...
no stress now...

The gods are not troubled
and do not trouble us.

... What mirrors!
... to help us

overlook... the world gnawing
(at us) like a rabid skunk gnaws

its own paw off in a trap...
gnaws (at us) as we watch

people getting rich
by making other people sick...

there but for the grace... give us strength
to help... despite...

... enough small pains of our own to wear us away...
... living lives of minor torture...

great disaster... But we can,
even with our body's woes,

look the other way again,
see the horses in the distant fields

admire hawks, and so forget
and turn the other cheek

for a kiss... find peace
for a while in the only now...

be useful... train ourselves... see it
another way... Mystery

gives back... the mystery
of compassion's pleasure...

The pain of fear and anger... can...
disappear... in a blink... of new attention.

All wisdom has understood
... the misery that we cause ourselves

adds misery to the world
and that is why the error

of indulging pain
with servile... rapt devotion...

befouls our peace
... stains the hope of others...

and, like despair,
is just no good.

(2012)

Five Temperaments of Now
Fragments from the Christmas Notebooks

Prologue

> *Now is a holy place.*

What a problem now is. What a puzzle.

Is now a particle or is it a wave,
or is it both
in a wild order hidden in a tangle?

Is it true that everything is,
and only is, in the now?

How do we base a life on something
that is once and over eternally?

It might as well be nothing
even though it is all.

This is not absurd.
But it's not very secure.

Why even think about now?
Because it is the only refuge,
the only safe place,
the only place that is.

The gift of new life
is always waiting to be found
just where we haven't looked.

I. Prison Break

Freedom is nothing but a chance to be better.

– Albert Camus

The warden, the dominating normal,
wants you to be predictable too.
It's easier if you are unhappy with yourself
but unclear why, fidgety.

But when you first see a moment of joy
deflect around you and speed off
like a spark darts with a breeze
you know you have become repellent

to the humor of the cosmos,
the humor reason tells us must
shadow love as a property
of atoms, space-time, quantum jest.

It's not just all fire, death, lies, and pain.
And you see you need upheaval.
You need to go into the streets of your life
and trust disillusion.

Better to limp away free,
at risk of your life, than to stay
dying of your sanity.

II. Not Missing a Thing

Wisdom comes by disillusionment.

– George Santayana

With the gift of crisis we can be
disillusioned by our certainties,
wise up and escape, this once, the *cloaca*
maxima of history flushing and perhaps

poke around in reality for a while,
with all its terrible teeth dripping gore and gristle
and, then, do the wise thing
— incapable of truth, victories, or martyrdom —
and ask yourself what can I do that won't disillusion me
with myself? What IS left to do.

Change is the gift.

We are called to do what we must
so we can't say at the end
"Oh no, I wasn't true. I did not do
my only self as I had hoped to do."

It's a liberty to be disillusioned with our caution,
our stubbornness, our cunning to avoid
what is hard and real to do.
Far from the day, in frozen deep night afraid,
you know you're still alive if you can't help but refuse
to waste the sleepless aching void and choose instead
to imagine all your cherished secret pleasures still ahead.

III. Ignoring or Attending

*Choice of attention — to pay attention to this
and ignore that — is to the inner life what
action is to the outer.*

— W. H. Auden

The inner battle is where hope is hidden,
this terrible strain with focus,
with what the Zen boss ordered when he yelled
"Pay attention!" But to what?

And you see that you don't have to be unrequited.
Just moving your eyes, just seeing
something else releases choice
to be an instrument of will and desire.

You are what you think about.
And if you think you can, you're right.
Let's be free of the stories that bring us to our knees.
We will see that what we want
and what we think about
are often not the same, and we must change.

Why not try
to refuse
to be unhappy
just this once?
Why not change
what makes you want to change?
Why not get out of your own way?

IV. Choreography of Time

To understand is to perceive patterns.

– Isaiah Berlin

Disruption is a gift that shows
patterns dance with us through time.
Some tangos even have
deep triggers of self-doubt,
pulled day in and day out.

Wisdom is in knowing what to overlook.
Just be sure not to miss the iceberg of hubris, right there.
It happens every time.
Say to yourself things are fixed or going right
and they will trample you and burn you like
your pet dragon would, scratching at an itch.

Be self-confident and you'll glide sometimes.
Be over-confident and you will trip into oblivion.

Change is the gift.
Stubbornness is not a pattern.
Friendly failings never work.
Refusal and denial can't dance a lick.

Unrepeatable patterns,
each unique, each disappearing,
are not cement blocks
hardening on your feet.

In a bar alone, you can feel sometimes
your disillusion fade and calm so you can take
the moon for a guide, bright, full, unmarred
among the velds of spotless abstract stars.

V. Love Drunk

Love shook my heart
like the wind on the mountain
rushing over the oak trees.

– Sappho

You spot her down the hall and see
just the bare silhouette of her form
and get flushed, breathe harder,
gulp air deeper, happier, amazed.

You see the trees now swaying,
woodwinds in the twilight, winter limbs
black lace against the sky.

Between rapture and despair, choose rapture, please.
No use to be so full of thoughts
you can't get love drunk on the chances of the day,
overwhelming, rocked back, dizzy sweet with it.

Now, go ahead, mistrust disillusion.

Love opens the rocky geode with a kiss,
the Milky Way explodes
like the first tongue tip on your lips.
Love makes the universe itself

feel warm as the small of her back,
as you stand before the stars,
glorious as they are, no more, though,
than her hand in yours. Content
and thrilled to roam the mind's eye as it sees
days ahead in calm, charmed patterns from afar.

Epilogue

The sacred and profane are sacred.

If now is how it works,
now is the gift we must receive.

And so new life each day
can always be where you find it
when you're not looking for it,
startling as a star path
on the bitter, midnight sea.

Angelic orders know
the anthem of perfection
as humans know the jive and joke
of now and then, and all over again
and again and again, nothing and everything,
zero and all.

But in the meantime, need we say,
in-between time, may we affirm,
before we're done,
what's the use of it
if we can't proclaim:
Oh joy almighty,
ain't we got fun!

(2013)

Six Liberties of Compassion

I. Restraint

Are we all prophets without honor
in the homeland of our inner lives,
weeping Jeremiahs haranguing

our resentments, pathetic outbursts,
sly lusts, our sweet teeth chattering?
What a joy it would be to have no need

of self-restraint. To be so true to life
that we are, with ease, just right.
But we know restraint's a tease.

Habits we deplore rule us without effort.
The sympathy we feel for our lonely better selves
disperses without mercy until we think we are

fated to be the objects of our self-derision,
destined to sculpt our ideal selves from blocks of marble
using only toothpicks like a million monkeys might.

But we go stale without prevailing
until some sainted rascal of restraint
whispers in our ear the rule of joy

we all can follow without fail:
Kindness is such an easy lesson to be learned
because it is so easy to return.

II. Becoming

We perceive and we imagine all at once.
No observation is without opinion.
The galaxies in their glory are not glorious to all.

Black holes are irresistible to those depressed,
swallowing light to prove that chemistry is a destiny
we can't escape. We're never free of who we are.

"We believe and we become."
The cat dies and we fall apart, as if the whole world
had crashed into another world we didn't see.

In the same way that death can never be wrong,
there cannot be an inside without an outside,
a before without a now and a now without an after.

Just born, just dead, we are timeless in between.
Becoming new is how we see it.
Everything's easy if you want it to be,

even dying on the vine, even falling into a crack
in the memory of the times. Imagination
lasts and lasts: it's what we do with who we are.

We don't need a Virgil to teach us our little hells.
Kindness is such an easy lesson to be learned
because it is so easy to return.

III. Empathy

When the caverns of our consciousness,
dark as the void the stars invade, transform into
sewers of hate or fear, when radiant interiors,

filled with forms of things unknown, become for each
a cloaca for the roaring Shadow of the Age,
empathy as compassion, a gift to all,

dulls into an empathy of us and them,
forcing some to scrub the streets on their knees,
while others are given the golden peace

of living without fear gnawing at their faces.
When empathy excludes, adoring some
as soapy babies, boiling others in pits

of blame they don't deserve,
when we cannot cut all others
the same slack we cut ourselves,

we become vaults slammed shut and locked.
Hope bounces off us like a hammer on a block of steel,
the holy monsters of the mind make caves of wonder

into bowels of pain — we must choose which one prevails.
Kindness is such an easy lesson to be learned,
because it is so easy to return.

IV. Euphoria

Epiphanies of glee, of unexplainable joy,
our sense that life is our perfect fate,
rapturous and overwhelmed on deadly cliffs,

staring out into the desert hopeless as the sky
and knowing we are nothing more or less
that Everything that is, atom born — these euphorias

come to us like our first escapes on bikes
up summer streets when we were eight.
Such inner soundings of belonging

turn the world from right and wrong
into the freedom of trust without an answer.
And we feel the cosmos that's within us,

the Exactly Who we are, wants to give
itself through us to the Everything Else that is
in which nothing is out of place, not even our judgment of it.

The whole mystery left to us is learning how to live
true to the perishable Only Once we are, adding the best
that we can be, that Never Again, to the whole of the All

before the end comes our way. Desiring the goal
is what truly matters. Kindness is such an easy lesson
to be learned, because it is so easy to return.

V. Friendship

It took one word and she knew
exactly what I meant. Old friends in love
are a culture of two, a tribe on a lonely veld

where languages spring up like shadows
that define, unique codes of inside jokes, taboos,
"you had to be there" ways of being true.

We are a form our freedom takes. We know
what to say and what not to say,
and when and where to say it and to not.

It takes a look, one shift of the shoulder, one
glancing off at the tree tops to say
a sonnet worth of sympathy

in an exhalation of relief — like loyalty
through the slippery wobblings of accident
and history's trap teaches us to understand

the echoes of our inner lives that sound
between us, as real as when we have befriended
who we are, ourselves, without constraint.

Banish accusation and unrequited gloom.
Kindness is such an easy lesson to be learned
because it is so easy to return.

VI. The Map of Joy

We chart our lives disaster by disaster, through cycles
of declining ages, the evidence of death and war.
We hardly ever build the map of joy with trails of ecstasy,
elation, moments filled to the brim with satisfaction,
admiration, boundless happiness in knowing, now at last,
the compassion of joy is nothing less
        than a cosmic truth for all — like the day
when you felt in your cells the universe was simply just
the way it was, and nothing could go wrong with anything,
        like the day your mother plucked you out from school,
sipped sodas with you by the sea, and you felt fully
and completely loved by the goddess,
        the moment when the secret life of the world
was shown to you in a paper bag with a geode
opened up inside, or the first time you fell madly in love
        with the scent of hot sunshine on bare
pine needles one afternoon when you were four.
Our joys define us more that our calamities,
        the hells of the world that we let in,
but our wiring treats happiness as a cheap thrill
and grief as a catechism of life and death.
        The body just plays the deep strings of sorrow
to prepare us for letting go. And when we chart
the course of our lives by the constellations of our joys, we see
        the true message of the mystery that the Books
have missed so badly in translation: that kindness is
an easy lesson to be learned, because it is so easy to return.

(2014)

Five Reasons Why Despair Is No Good

The First Reason: Love

Love is the rock, the law, the final refuge
as killing slithers all around us. It's our only chance.

Who you ache for, who you're made for,
whose pain you cannot bear, whose joy wipes out
the bleakest pout, that soul, idea, community
you'd flat out die for — that's the surest clue
to peace upon this earth.
                                        Love is not elusive,
not beyond us, not only a miracle of coincidence,
or fate's blind whim. We can come to it ourselves.
It's the way to a sympathy that's in us from the start,
waiting for us to have the heart to dare to be more
than we're afraid we are.
                                        Despair is no good.
It slams the vault door shut, leaves love pounding
soundlessly, suffocating in the safe of a righteous
sadness we cannot escape. But love
picks all locks, can free itself from anything,
a virtuoso, as we know, at magic, opening even
rusty old hearts with a sleight of mind
that finds our sympathies no matter where
despair has worried out a place to hide them.

The Second Reason: Beauty

Beauty startles despair, a breath-taking
that can jolt even pain away.
How can gloom resist
the slope of Aphrodite's hips, moon smooth,
or rainbow seashells on black sand beaches
dazzling for mating, or a bright sea windy morning,
or jungle green profusions of beans and tomatoes,
or baby grins, the cat sidling up to the universe,
arcades of elms, fields of lavender,
a holy mountain as a neighbor, or that smile,
of all smiles, her face comforting and inspiring
with celestial grace.
Despair is a sobbing
in one's peace of mind. It is a giving up which means
beauty has abandoned the eye of the beholder,
the inner eye itself going blind to the mysteries
of music, of poetry, of galaxies and love, of pure logic rising
from $E = mc^2$.
That's why despair is no good.
It is an insult on a par with hubris
when we're brought so low from the pinnacles of pride.
Despair buries us alive in agonies of inattention.
It's not our heads in the sand, it's who we are,
ourselves, as creatures of the stars, stuck, dazed,
finished off like sea birds gummed up with tar.

The Third Reason: Wonder

Wonder, where all thinking starts,
abandons depression by taking up all the room.

How can despair get a grasp when you're marveling
at everything, at the brilliant persistence of ants,
at skin so smooth it feels warmly polished
by Aphrodite's sighs and kisses,
at pelicans gliding low above the waves,
at a masterpiece of clouds, the philodendron's
unfurling leaf, at the old cat's wild
escapading gallop down the hall?
                              Even despair at facts
of inhumanity and the cruelty of greed,
the whole snake pit side of consciousness, disappears
in the wake of amazement at any knowing of the holy
beyond the rank delusions of our hates and fears,
any knowing,
                    even humor's,
that standup version of wonder in the universe
so astounding, so beyond even death, the snatcher,
who has never laughed, so beyond infernos of atoms
that nothing sees coming — *hilaritas*, the joke,
the funny punch line on his big white charger,
rocking and shouting and jeering, saving the world,
triumphant, pickle nose flashing, shirt hanging out
his zipper as he prances along, dunce divine,
slashing at doom in his pink feathered slippers.

The Fourth Reason: Curiosity

Curiosity replaces judgment, which chokes out life
slowly with displeasure.
                         The world is
what you make of it, isn't it? And what you make of it
is built from what you know of it, is it not?
Isn't there always another way, always more
to be understood?
                         The question and its mark
are all the codes we need to crack the riddle
of our dungeon minds. Curiosity is its own
liberation.
                         Who do you believe? Is any of this true?
Is truth singular? Why does time go only forward?
What are dreams? How can I be happy if the world
around me is a cauldron of suffering and oppression?
If free will is a falsehood, why do we choose sometimes
to change our minds in favor of our better natures?
Is now determined solely by then,
by a brutal certainty with no variation from the rack
of absolute cause and effect?
                         Might not one day
some internal impulse of imagination take hold
in each of us, so we'd make a leap of being,
all of us together, to a world where love breeds curiosity
and all our questions abandon hatred
as superfluous and spoiled?

The Fifth Reason: Change

Change pulls the thread, unravels the false
logic of despair. Nothing, not even the worst,
doesn't end.
        Integrity evolves. We learn how to be
who we are at our best — yes, even that can happen.
The quicksand of our flaws can often be escaped
by just a gentle change of position.
We start with what we are given.
The rest is ours:
        the Infinitely Malleable, until despair
freezes change and fate's chokehold seizes our good humor
and rubs our noses in the mere rudeness
of reality, so defined.
        But what if a Goddess whispers
"Be who you are: Change: Relax."
Is that all it takes? Can we really learn
to ride waves of disappointment
without falling off so we can turn and try again?
Can we trust the fundamental element —
The Possible in its Enormity? Why not?
        Are we prone
to darkness? Yes. Does the world we describe
fall apart as we say it? Mostly. But despair knows,
wrongly, that chance won't budge. We all know ideals
morph into their bitter shadows.
        We all can reason, though,
that the mirror image of despair, its nameless opposite
marvelous with hope, must be there, somewhere,
waiting for us to change so we can find it.

(2015)

Cosmic Relief: Five Comic Slip-ups on the Road to Peace of Mind

Slip-up Number One: Reality

To fall or not to fall in the shower
that is the question, whether to suffer the dings
and knocks of outrageous flops or to admit
the universe likes a good laugh, that it really loves it
when you're sucker-punched by your own PR,
believing the world actually *is* what you're used to
and doesn't make change its universal solvent, that it loves
the mad race when you glance over your shoulder
and your worst nightmare flies past you on the other side
and finishes first. It's like the pratfall sneeze relief,
the soggy Kleenex that reveals O NO snot and guck
as real as the final whoopie stop,
the cold hard tile on your coccyx.
It's not unlike the moment you know
you can't keep up with the future any more
and stand on the sidewalk watching time race away
into a world without you as you fidget, looking
for a park bench and feel the weight of the eons
slip from you as fast as you slam to the soapy bottom
on your soapy bottom. But let's don't laugh at each other.
Hubris slams the door on the thumb you poke in your eye
while washing your face. By this time, though,
life has loosened you up and you're so cool, so slick
harm shoots from your grasp like a bar of soap.
Humor is so hygienic.

Slip-up Number Two: Reason

Catching a toe on the bottom stair
with a tray full of wine in long stem glasses,
tripping the quite fantastic, a tumbling high-flier,
your chin sideswipes the dusty
funny bone of the cosmos, so accident prone
it's banana peels all the way down to nada.
The mind likes to joke; it lets you think
it thinks it can fit the world into what it thinks.
And when its ideas are too small or silly
for the world to fit, reason reasons it can just
trim off what's hanging out like so much fat and gristle.
But some people remember, become heretics even,
nasty angels of equality, and what was trimmed begins
to undo even the most powerful reasoning of oppression.
That's why reason can't cut it, but myths and fairy tales can.
They aren't reasonable and so ideas like Zeus,
the loather of hubris, and Santa Claus,
the god of child delight, absolutes like Artemis,
Athena and Aphrodite never get trimmed off altogether.
Their little worm paths always remain.
And as you watch yourself tumble in air
like a Dali black cat hurtling into the ether, know that reason
hasn't caught up with you yet, that behind the looking glass,
the stand up cosmos tells the truth with a punch line in the eye;
ah, but your thumb is already there — strange victories;
laugh enough and the cosmos comes to know
that you're the guy in the front row it can always count on.
That won't get you much more than a wing and a prayer
but a miss is as good as a mile.

Slip-up Number Three: Truth

Boy that bathtub is slick and deep
almost as fathomless as knowing
what's fact and what's not,
and you a wispy bug falling off
the ring of grime. The universe laughs out loud
when you fall for the great joke of truth
that any hack attorney, any cop or comb-over
grandstander or rival colleague can talk you out of
what you know for sure by sowing just one or two
poppyseeds or other tiny spit wads of doubt
retrieved from their dentures. The truth,
even if disproven, is still soap scum on the lens
of knowing. Just say a lie, just make an accusation,
and those with mousetrap minds will snap it up
with lethal certainty. And nothing's more certain
than the horror inflicted by those
who are certain. They have their footing
for clambering out of the tub. But they always
crash hard, topple back then smack tied up
in knots, scrambling, inane. And when they finally
creep into bed, PJs wadded, nighties bunched,
wedgies all the way down,
the bruises too big to miss tossing and turning,
they rest in the certain conviction
they didn't really fall, that it was all
the bathtub's fault after all.

Slip-up Number Four: Logic

Stepping from the curb you see the bus won't stop
but your sharp old pal hauls you back by the jacket
just in time, just like you pull away the energy of worry
from breaking down into the jaws of corrupted logic
caught by absurd disguised errors in the premise,
rather like a blindsiding bus that will flatten you.
Yup, things like that break down into cosmic skits,
gangsters running governments, profiteers making fortunes
selling tragic junk food for thought to the angry,
forcing good people to imagine they actually know the good
when their knowledge is based on a comedy of slick mistakes
they've been sold like hotcakes.
Is there a lesson in error? Is logic an absurd tragedy deferred
if we see it in time? No, the world is not as it is
because it has to be, it is because it is not any other way
than it is at the moment. Could it be different,
could reflexes fail, logic jam up in the pipe
and explode in a mutually assured destruction?
Why not? It is not the best of all possible worlds,
or the worst quite yet. And you are there on the curb
when the bus flies past, safe as if smelling the roses,
tousle-haired by a zephyr clearing the air
on a sunny morning, hubris a shaggy pun,
and you grinning discreetly still just a groaner
smacking your lips, gulping down sweet humble pie.

Slip-up Number Five: Sanity

Tripped up by a crack in the sidewalk
you hear the cosmic comic chirp of approval
as you just miss slamming to the ground
like a lodge pole pine in the forest.
Thawoomp, and see, for no reason, that sanity
is not all it's cracked up to be, but a sort of shtick
with blowhard bullies proving ego and moral
self-soiling belong, like frackers all fracked up
on a methane high, to the cosmic comedy club
in the sky. Who's saner, really: the officer
obeying orders and pushing the button
of annihilation, the cop who shoots the crazy man
for threatening him with a butter knife,
the businessman who robs everyone blind
and is considered a genius when he's found out,
or the furry student philosopher
counting dandelions as a method
of peaceful devotion, the old folks who
refuse to even remember all the honors
of their lives, much less recount them,
the gentle harpist who can't find her car keys
day after day but makes everyone else
feel they're in heaven? Who's loony?
Accidents of history bloom so fast
you just have to assume that in the right
frame of mind, the crack in the sidewalk
and the kind person's smile could both
make you fall for life again.

(2016)

Five Things to Do When There's Nothing Left to Be Done

I. Find Something Impossible to Do

Romans painted oculi that opened
to blossoms flying in the sky.
It's not far-fetched to say
that in a different mind-land

in dreamy weather, you will remember
how you dug yourself out of the rubble,
how you held on when there was no reasoning
only loving left. Hurricanes, earthquakes,

bruised minds — you cannot solve them.
Just don't get trapped inside them.
It's usually you who are the source
of the unsolvable. Don't be dashed

and splattered by your own debris. We all
live in a labyrinth of musts, and in our own
labyrinth minds like darkrooms with blinking
"no exit" signs. It's the wisdom of lovers

to change the sheets, leverage her legs into bed,
help her softly with her underwear, make home
anywhere. Aphrodite knows all there is to know.
So don't mind, talk yourself free, innocent

as a fool trying gladly against the impossible.
There's only loving enough to survive
by learning how to be who you are at heart
more than you ever knew before you absolutely had to.

II. Seek Impossible Pleasures

Sorrows scudding, cloudy passions
curling wave after wave, lullabies of tides,
a world of beaches, gulls strutting,
gliding off on the wind. Everything's gone.

Don't be afraid to be a kid. That's where
the mind-land can present a kinder place,
if you've trained it, a pretend world
of iced raspberries and gin, days in the big chair

reading the pain away, a world
that's only different because you know
it is pretend. When all that's left is accepting
that silence has a rapture of its own,

you know the wisdom of explorers
traveling always on the edge of information.
No territory is devoid of its astonishments,
euphorias, some perfect rock that says it all.

Focusing on what hasn't gone all wrong quite yet,
you in dreamy awe absorbed, not minding
makes counting your breaths a rhapsody
in a homecoming of pretend, the evenings

radiant with clear warmth, hot bread, butter,
slow-cooked conversation in the winter freeze, insight
warm as goose down, like you saying thanks
even for the end because you cannot help but mean it.

III. Keep the Heavy Door from Slamming Shut

When you've left the key inside,
and you always might, leave the big door ajar,
don't write anything off, you never know.
The wisdom of dogs and cats tells us so.

Cats: Make them want you, give them only
the exactly real, you can't help it. You know
they always love it. Dogs: Do unto them what *they*
want you to do unto them. They want to be adored,

yearned for, thrilled at being seen, so why not
give it? Wisdom says false hope is a farce.
When patterns are aligned, though, and history decrees
what usually happens next, you hear

the big door click shut. Ah, but you remembered
to take the key. And so you have grown small again,
a dream child moving through the land
as worlds fall apart so they can create

the out-of-the-blue forever. Grief, itself, gives
freedom from the fear of grief. And even now,
with cataracts like foggy mornings on the beach,
even now you can see that fun,

the darling goddess, is to stress
what sunlight is to ice.
Oh, be a sun bather whatever the weather.
But do keep an eye on the door.

IV. Be Impossibly Grown Up

The infallible pleasure of juggling fire,
how can we stop, even though we are
admonished to take care of ourselves,
to put the oxygen mask on first.

But no one tells us how
to thwart our instincts. We trust the truth
is almost never straight ahead
or around the next corner even. Who knew

that relief of pressure would be such
an impossible pleasure? Want peace
in a state of madness? Don't force it.

That's the wisdom of those who make
new things out of themselves. They wait
to see what shows up, appears through the pen,
out the pencil. They go along, indulge the possible.

Don't give madness anything to push against
and rejoice that the known can do no worse.
Chaos solves itself, like a poem appears on the page,
like water finds a downward slope,

or sand finds a fissure to fill. Play like that
in dreamy joy. Think, get on with living, find out
how to get home. Take the painful risk. Patience,
patience is the other universal solvent.

V. Make Offerings to Hilaritas

for TH, Buffgies, Michelle, and Henry

The joke's on us. We knew it all along. Do funny,
get ahead of the game, only with the best of friends
indulge in verbal quackery and that kind of thing,
and things of that nature, and so forth and so on

and stuff like that. There are no words for life
and such like. So when you put too fine a point on it,
you miss the point altogether. It's like a diagnosis,
definition's always in doc speak, insurance jargon,

and whatnot. Happiness depends on what you do
with what you know. Wisdom is often
all that's left. The funny thing with words
is that some of them actually do

say what they mean, but miss what your meaning
refers to. Dreamy fun will do. The funny bone plays its tune
on a skeleton xylophone out of tune. But anything is funny,
even stuff like this if your sense of humor isn't locked

in your private sense of doom. Now there's a word
— doom. It's always *all* up to you.
Fun is to innocence what love is to grief.
Lost memory is overwhelmed by love unforgotten.

Fall off your fear with a galloping thud. You're always
giving the speech with your shirt caught in your zipper.
Homesick? Even unto death? It ends so soon and so forth.
Don't mind. No one remembers the punch line anyway.

(2017)

Five Treasure Maps to the Labyrinth of Trust

Map Number One: Knowing What You Know

That's the vine tossed to you in the quicksand of self-pity
as you tread suction in a morass of laughs.
That kind of knowledge comes from having a feel
        for the invisible. The palm-sized crystal globe
        shows more than a circle. It lets you know,
        with your own eyes, the inside is real
even if you can't see all of it. So what do you trust?

You are certain you exist, even if you must
        doubt your certainty. You know for sure
        you don't know enough. You know the cosmos
        cannot be some sick joke played on the sentient
by a ludicrous devil god anymore than it can be
        a passing thought in the Mind of the Divine. Or can it?
        You know that love is the only thing that bears

no possibility of guilt, in itself. You know when you are lost.
You know the invisible is the way the mystery appears,
as when a living thing dies, it's merely a pile of parts
        no science can revive. You know that kindness is right
        and cruelty is wrong, that love is the truth.
        You know, it turns out, quite a lot.
But can you find your way out?

Map Number Two: Doubt as Evidence

Doubt is the flying trapeze between
    what you think you know and what actually is.
It's the best way across and it's always without a net.
Losing your way is not a tragic circus act, if you make the catch.
    It leads to getting found, to finding out
for yourself how to fly, free of delusions of grace. Even if
    the scalpel of doubt is sharpened

only to butter knife standards, it can still slice
    though the stink of hate. When something
doesn't add up, like saying a puma skull is where
all its catness lay, as if a cat was invulnerable to its prey,
    or when a specialist generalizes absolute truth
we take that as a ludicrous self-deception,
    malign balderdash. We leave the room

when a poppycock general, protesting goodness too much,
    tries to make us doubt what doubt has taught us.
Doubt too much, not too little. But never doubt
the paradoxes that do you in. Doubt doubts itself.
    You can trust it until it becomes your standard response.
Then unlock the cage, and let it flap and growl its way
    over the labyrinth and escape all the rules.

Map Number Three: Revulsion and Attraction

It is not up to us, our gag reflex can't be denied.
We can't swallow political maggots
or swindling rats in our food. We can't stomach sadism,
hate rancid propaganda. Revulsion is a faultless map.
Attraction starts the same, it's just easier to lose your way
than it is to be found. That dinosaur turd of your dad's,
it looks like it's wet and stinks, but when you touch it

it's a stone, a coprolite, an object of abject fascination
to a child, shit keeping its form for millions of years.
When repulsed you flee. The doctor who labels you at a glance
and treats you like a quick description,
shun him like you would a dinosaur shitting.
With attraction, if you trust the gravity of it, the helplessness
of its powers, being pulled inexorably,

then attraction is as grave as falling. It goads possession,
the old slapstick of confusing having with being.
You must see if who you are attracted to is attracted to you,
what kind of closeness is compelled.
You trust it, how could you not? It is gravity after all.
But to be safe you must wait in the maze to see how fast
empathy finds the pathway too, and if it's looking for you.

Map Number Four: Intuiting Up and Down

High-wire dancing, the inner gyroscope cuts you no slack,
reveals time's razor line getting lost in plain sight.
    You can feel life and death with the soles of your feet.
    But vertigo sets in. Something's taking you under,
a riptide of more than depression — and it comes to you
that this down is dangerous and that the bottom
    is too far down. You must stop minding. It's not unlike

trusting your fathomless sadness sinks with perpetual fear
coming true in the end, fear the clairvoyant, like a shark
    as a chaperone, thrashing at the bottom, not knowing
    up from down. When it comes to survival,
you don't need hard evidence. Like when you're told
thought is a sparkling secretion and love a tango of molecules,
    not metaphorically, but neurologically for real,

you sense the powerful have purged doubt from themselves.
You are your own seeing-eye dog.
    You know that intuition is
    catching the right scent among the millions
of stray aromas — hey, there's a bear right around the corner,
over there an angel is just about to tell you sweetly what not to do.
    That you can take into battle.

Map Number Five: Love as Gravity

Love is unquestioned, undoubted, irrefutable.
It is losing the way to being lost. It has no opposite.
It trusts you to be who you are. Hate is not on its spectrum.
Standing on the rim of the Milky Way, or the precipice
    before the fossil sea bed of canyons and spires,
    seeing your grandchildren smile, the warm eyes
of your lover, she whose love was the equal sign

    that joined the best of you to the rest of everything —
    those are maps that *are* the territory just as being
bowled over by Bach in the garden is, or holding the stone
with stratigraphy of eons in the palm of your hand,
    as is your admiration of time and what it makes —
    the 300-million-year-old seashell replaced
with fool's gold so precise and perfect without intent,

    it makes you laugh with longing. So many
    treasure maps to the sublime. The labyrinth of trust
ends and begins by looking yourself straight in the eye.
Like finally being allowed to speak her native tongue,
    the connoisseur of clouds cannot help but find herself
    in love with the goodness that made her know
that any love is good.

(2018)

Five Innocent Merriments
of Being in Love Again with Being Alive

I. Dancing with Time

Entropy dismantles everything. Nothing is spared,
vibrant life or crooked malice. Our homes
run down, so does our despair and the intolerable
sufferings of fear. Confidence wanes and joy
can play itself out, but so does terror, exquisite pain.
The single truth that change never touches,
until it's all over, is the mystery of
perpetual emotion, the spontaneous new,
infinite jolt of falling in love with being alive.
Even entropy itself runs out of gas. Only
the gravity of love changes without
diminishment as the everlasting source

of goodness that entropy clears the way
to refresh, again and again, never ceasing.

II. It Loves You Back

When you fall in love with being alive,
life loves you back. What doesn't love
to be loved? What doesn't feel humbled
and ecstatic with the luck of not being left
unrequited? Love the sun and it lets you see
its green and growing edge moving through
the darkest human history like a forest moves
renewed across an ashen void. Falling in love
smooths flaws, sees genius in oddity, morphs
blemishes and bulges into sweet slopes and curves,
restores trust and withers grudges with just
the fascination, the single focus

of adoring curiosity. And life itself
always knows it, and gives you back all it's got.

III. Not a Sick Joke

So many 2x4s careening through the fog of chance
— is this a cosmic sick joke played out in the rumpus
room galaxy of an infernal brat? It's not credible
that the entirety of it all is a prank and the mind
a shaggy dog story with homicidal malice.
It just doesn't compute. Is it all without value
when the cosmos creates in us the expectation
of value? Focus, she always said, on what
doesn't hurt. Forbear, adore, fall in love
and you will see all the rest, what's not
disordered, like you would see your child,
your lover, the mountains, a stormy sky,

see the cosmos like that, as a cherished soul
not a perverse, random and vindictive pest.

IV. Too Beautiful to Resist

Dawn light opalized through mountain cold,
how can you resist the bare beauty of the world
once you see it, once you know it will be everywhere
you choose to look, if you choose to look? How can you
resist falling in love with everything
beautiful and kind, compassionate in its strength,
how can you resist touching the smooth,
long flow of time as if it were warm sea foam
around your ankles, or over there, running
through the meadow, shooting stars
invisible around her, daughter of the weather,
grand in her childhood and in her blood bond

with you, the gift of generations — how can you resist
falling in love again with being alive?

V. Splendor, Mirth, and Good Cheer

Being in love, we can see the truth of life
for what it is as it happens. Imperfection, pain,
blindsiding bad luck, all exist in spacetime
as fun does, as flesh-and-blood hope,
mirth, and quanta darting and effervescing do.
It's all inconceivably pointless and purposeful
without end. Is pain more powerful than humor?
Is irony more truthful than skin-and-bone love?
If misery is more convincing than warm breezes,
of course suicide is the only rebuttal. But add up
the totals. Cruelty and evil exist. They are random
shrapnel shredding peace for a while, but are not

equal in power to the gentleness they disquiet
as they vanish passing through.

(2019)

About the author

V. B. Price has been working to repair his ignorance since he came to New Mexico in 1958 at the age of 18. He studied anthropology and philosophy at the University of New Mexico and has been publishing poetry since 1962. He's worked continuously as a reporter and an environmental and political columnist for 54 years. His column currently runs weekly at mercmessenger.com. He had the great privilege of teaching at UNM's School of Architecture and Planning and in UNM's Honors College for more than three decades. His books include *Chaco Trilogy*, *Memoirs of the World in Ten Fragments*, *The Orphaned Land: New Mexico's Environment Since the Manhattan Project*, *Mythwaking*, *The Seven Deadly Sins*, and *Albuquerque: A City at the End of the World*.

His father once called him "fortune's child." The vast luck of his life is embodied in his children, his grandchildren, and in the landscape of his beloveds both in the ground and still walking upon it. His good fortune blossoms in the students who have mentored him, the friends who have taught him, and in New Mexico who has mothered him.

Casa Urraca Press

We are a home for words that speak to the soul and stimulate thought. We publish daring, eloquent authors of poetry and creative nonfiction. And we offer workshops with our authors and other artists.

Every writer and every publisher has a slant. Ours tilts toward the richness of the high desert, where all are welcome who manage to find their way.

Proudly centered somewhere near Abiquiu, New Mexico.

Visit us at casaurracaltd.com for exquisite editions of our books, and for workshop registration.

Lightning Source UK Ltd.
Milton Keynes UK
UKHW010713260123
416005UK00004B/272